THE
RADICAL
REMNANT

Rick Warzywak

ACKNOWLEDGEMENTS

I want to thank my wife Barbara for being at my side all these years. She has been a great help and support to me. I am so blessed to be married to the wife of my youth. It will be until death do us part. I also thank my children Amanda, Matthew, Megan and Micah for always being so supportive after I had entered full time ministry in 1990. They are arrows shot out to impact the world for God's kingdom purposes.

I am appreciative to the many fine Bible teachers that have crossed my path and sowed into my life. It is their teaching and instruction that enabled me to glean so much over the years. I am also thankful to the many friends and family that have invested in my ministry over the years financially and with prayerful support.

Finally, what would I be like without Christ as my Savior? I am thankful to have a directed purpose and destiny that comes out of a personal relationship with the Lord Jesus Christ. Eternity is before us and to see the hope we have in Him is such a blessing.

Contents

INTRODUCTION

Do you feel it? Have you ever had a feeling that history is at a crossroads? We are experiencing a present day shaking in the world. There is something that is crying out in many saying what can we do? What must I personally do? How can we bring Godly change? People are being stirred across America hearing these same questions. Amidst the adversity and pessimism there is a *radical remnant* that is being called. I am being awakened to the fact that God wants to use me. He is calling out *modern day circuit riders* sounding the alarm saying all is not lost. You are a circuit rider! We can turn America around and be a righteous nation. This is no time to be apathetic or slumbering.

> **Point to Ponder:** "I believe it is the best of times and for those without faith—it is the worst of times. The glory and the shaking come together. It is true on both sides of the coin. We are crossing the threshold into the Third Great Awakening and yet we are crossing the threshold into a great Worldwide Shaking." - Jim Goll

A sleeping church is awakening as the importance of prayer is coming to the forefront. Individuals are being prompted by the Holy Spirit to pro-actively engage the culture. There is an excitement in the air. Vision and purpose is being released. God is handing out assignments to each of us and people are listening to that still small voice that is thundering across our land. The pieces of a puzzle are on the table and falling into place. We are the pieces of God's plan so allow Him to position us. Let him connect the dots and network

His people. The body of Christ is coming together as one and God's house will be a united house of prayer. This revelation from the throne of God is being discovered again. **The <u>Lamb</u> who became the <u>Lion</u> is on the move. The prayer closet is being pursued by those who are yearning for more of God.** It is only prayer that will build relationship and release the favor of God.

> **Point to Ponder:** "God does nothing except in response to believing prayer."

The good news is that increasing levels of personal and corporate prayer are being birthed across America. The church is beginning to respond and prayer as incense is rising up to God. The promptings of the Holy Spirit to pray are being heeded by His church. There is a **"great awakening baby"** in the birth canal of America. The praying *radical remnant* are initiating the contractions to birth this child. We declare and proclaim America will be saved!

Rick Warzywak

• 1 •

THE RADICAL REMNANT

God is calling out His *"radical remnant"* so the kingdom of Heaven can invade earth. We are in a season of Divine opportunity where God desires to intervene in our behalf. It is a historic time. We can be thankful that God has chosen each of us to be potential history makers. Are you saying I can change the course of history? Yes! This *radical blistering hot remnant* has a calling and destiny for these end times. God has always set aside a people who are hot in pursuit of Him. This remnant will carry out His end time assignment. The challenge is who will respond in this last days battle?

"Yet I reserve seven thousand in Israel – all whose knees have not bowed down to Baal and all whose mouths have not kissed him." **(2 Kings 19:18)**

Re-discovering the place where we can hear His voice is the lost jewel in the throne room of God. It is being revealed again to the few who are listening—*the radical remnant*. In this place the Holy Spirit of God will give us peace and calm. It is a place where God will enlarge our hearts to be able to carry out His marching orders. Divine remedies will manifest where we will be able to impact our sphere of influence. Yes, we will be challenged in this place. In this secret place of personal prayer we will be questioned deep down in our own spirits. Every individual, church and region is now faced with a choice of light or darkness, revival or judgment. The *radical remnant* in the prayer closet will decide the fate of each region.

Point to Ponder: "Satan does not care how many people read about prayer but if only he can keep them from praying. - Paul E. Billheimer

Do we want revival or judgment? I desire revival for my family, church, city, county, state and nation. We are a nation that can be transformed and awakened. He has provided a window of opportunity for the church of Jesus Christ to rise up and take its place. All the pieces are in place for a visitation of God upon our land. Each region must make that choice as increasing waves of challenges are flooding the land. Some may call it a perfect storm or say it is judgment. Others say God is providing a door to step through so the church can take its true place. The kingdom of Heaven is at hand and we are the ones to facilitate its coming.

Point to Ponder: "It is likewise interesting the alignments that are now taking place. In the church, there are gatherings of believers from almost across the spectrum of denominations and movements who want to join together, not in a denominational organization, but as different groups who have a common enemy, a common threat to their existence. There are non-religious groups who want to join with the religious because of the overwhelming threat of evil they perceive. It is truly a remarkable time, and it seems that the **greatest of all battles between good and evil is now unfolding,** and we get to be in it!" - Rick Joyner

We have entered into a season of time in history that is unprecedented. How many times have you heard that before? Every year that passes seems to be the crossroad year. We are at a crossroad for the existence of America and the freedoms we so endear. The only way to meet the challenge today is for the church to take its rightful place and **stand in the gap for the land.** America must choose the path of righteousness. Our nation is in desperate need in this hour as we are facing many difficulties. No human remedy will suffice. It will take *"Divine Intervention"* and nothing else to provide the cure for the ills that are upon us. We are feeling the effects of what has manifested in our land over the past decades. Some of us are being impacted directly while others indirectly.

Point to Ponder: "Several established prophets are declaring that the "Perfect Storm" is coming or even upon us. In 1987, the Lord showed me part of what would take place in the year 2010, and I remember it all so well. The Holy Spirit spoke to me in the night seasons that the world would begin to unravel in 2010, and it would be a hinge in world history where things would never return to what we have considered normal. In 1987 the Holy Spirit showed me that 2010 would be the beginning of the TIME OF GREAT STORMS. It is upon us!"
- Jim Goll

Throughout history even in the most difficult times there has been a *radical remnant* who had overcome adversity by faith. They had chosen to adhere to the promises of God which resulted in His blessings. This radical remnant exists here today. They are being called out as God has preserved them. They have a desire to draw closer to God. They long for the glory of God to come upon the earth. This remnant understands the importance of nurturing a relationship with the king of kings the Lord Jesus Christ. They are the champions.

*"But now I will not treat **the remnant** of this people as in the former days,' says the Lord of hosts. For the seed shall be prosperous, the vine shall give its fruit ,the ground shall give her increase, and the heavens shall give their dew — **I will cause the remnant of this people** to possess all these. And it shall come to pass that just as you were a curse among the nations, O house of Judah and house of Israel, so I will save you, and you shall be a blessing. Do not fear, let your hands be strong."* (**Zechariah 8: 11-13**)

This *radical remnant* understands that seeking God in the secret place (personal prayer) is where directions and purpose of life is given. The prayer closet is where the voice of God is heard and we can walk in full confidence by faith (2 Corinthians 5:7). It is where He orders and directs our steps (Proverbs 16:9). As I turn on the news each day I think what will be the next challenge our nation must face. There is a realization within that **human remedy cannot solve these problems.** But, God gives His *radical remnant* assurance as we abide in Him. As the world shakes and is flooded with a tsunami of challenges this praying remnant is covered with the peace of God. We have this peace even in the impact historic moments that are manifesting with increasing rapidity. The prayer closet is the place where we are able to sink spiritual roots so deep that when the earth shakes the "tree of life" will never be uprooted. Sink your roots as an Oak tree! You can be an Oak of righteousness and bring hope to those around you (Isaiah 61:3 – NIV).

Point to Ponder: "As in the movie The Perfect Storm, the storm I see coming to the United States is a combination of more than one element, and when the elements unite, the storm becomes exponentially more dangerous. However, unlike the movie, this storm is not just a storm of merging weather patterns. This storm is worse; it involves 5 different elements: religion, politics, economics, war, and geo-physical events. Massive problems in these five areas will come often, or in combination, and sometimes repeatedly. Each element has potentially several events that will have national and international ripple effects. Some ripples will be worse than others, depending on where you live and how you make your living. Different areas of the United States will experience different severities. Some will experience more economic elements, others more geo-physical elements; some will experience all elements. Remember, it is the combination and the rapidity that will make the storm problematic." - John Paul Jackson

---

Impact Moments

We have entered a time now where all will be affected by unfolding events that will be considered as **"impact moments"**. What is an impact moment? Think back when 9-11 struck America, and the Trade Towers were taken down by an act of terrorism. Where were you at that time? Can you recall the day and actually trace your steps of what you did? I was in a motel lobby in Midland, MI waiting to go preach the Gospel on a university campus. I watched the events unfold on a TV station in the lobby. As a seventh grader when President John F. Kennedy was assassinated I can remember being at home with the flu in bed watching history unfold. These are impact moments. **We have entered a time where impact moments will be increasing.**

> **Point to Ponder:** "We have to pray with our eyes on God, not on the difficulties." - Oswald Chambers

The political, economic, geophysical, social, church, family and educational realms are facing challenges that will shake every foundation on which we rested them. The earth is shaking and groaning. Economic unrest, pandemics and the threats of terrorism are increasing. There is only one foundation to build on that will survive the shakings in these coming years and that is Jesus Christ. The **voice of the Lord is shaking the wilderness** (Psalm 29:8). We have entered a <u>perfect</u> <u>storm</u> where simultaneous challenges in the world are coming together as one. God is moving and attempting to wake up the church. For those who walk by faith it is the best of times and for those without it will be the worst of times. **You are an awakened one who walks by faith.** The praying *radical remnant* is alive and well. So what is the hope? What must the church do? Is this nation able to turn back to God in such a way where another "Great Awakening" can occur in America? Do we have a choice in the late hour we are facing? These questions can all be answered as God prefers mercy over judgment (Psalm 103:8).

It rests on a people who will rise up and pray with a **renewed** **<u>desperation.</u>** We face the challenge of returning to a place where God will restore His favor. It is called the dwelling place of God. God's presence in the times we are in is the only solution. We must keep the *fire on the altar of prayer* burning (Exodus 29:41-43). This is the answer! May we seek the Lord and receive His divine refuge and strength **in the prayer closet (Matthew 6:6) or secret place (Psalm 91:1).** The *radical remnant* must rise up and go to work.

> **Point to Ponder:** "God shapes the world by prayer. The more prayer there is in the world the better the world will be, the mightier the forces of good against evil ..." - E.M. Bounds

• 2 •

HERRNHUT CHANGED HISTORY

What is Herrnhut? Why is this name so significant and symbolic today? The name means <u>watch</u> <u>of</u> <u>the</u> <u>Lord.</u> This prayer movement began in 1727 and helped birth the "Great Awakening" in America. It began with twenty people (*radical remnant*) who have released the favor of God upon what they had desired to accomplish.

> **Point to Ponder:** Those who ignore history are doomed to repeat it. Those who ignore history will never know how to advance beyond it. Study and learn to glean from the good from past history and utilize it as a model for the future.

Herrnhut was birthed from prophetic word that was spoken. Many important historical moments had manifested from a dream, vision, or a visitation from God. The promise will come and is usually birthed out of hardship and persecution. I have found that every demotion is an opportunity for promotion. Every wound or hardship can be currency in Heaven and spent for God's Kingdom purposes. Spiritual authority is given to those who understand persecution, betrayal, hurts, setbacks, and being treated unfairly. The secret is overcoming our adversities by trusting in God, walking in forgiveness, love and humility.

Joseph was an example (Genesis Chapters 37-48). God gave him a dream that was filled with promise and spoke of Joseph's greatness.

But there was a price to pay. Trials and tests came. His brothers turned on him and sold him into slavery to the Ishmaelites because of their hatred and jealousy. After being sold in Egypt by the Ishmaelites to Potiphar (an officer of Pharaoh) he gained favor and authority. Then the wife of Pharaoh attempted to seduce him and he withstood the temptation. She falsely accused him and he was put into prison. Joseph was given favor with the keeper of the prison which led to him interpreting the dreams of the chief butler and baker who were in prison. After Pharaoh had some disturbing dreams the chief butler spoke to him about Joseph. Joseph eventually interpreted the dreams of Pharaoh (after two years of imprisonment) and gained the favor of Pharaoh. Joseph was appointed second in command over Egypt. All of this did not come easily as Joseph had to pay a price of self sacrifice.

The Moravians faced much persecution throughout history which led to Herrnhut. The Moravian movement began with Christian Martyr John Hus being burned at the stake in the 1400's. Read this account of Herrnhut below and may hope rise up out of the desperate circumstance you may be facing. The answer to change America and save our nation is recorded in history. Can we learn from lessons in the past? I believe we can as the *radical remnant* is surfacing. He wants to use each of us.

Herrnhut – Impacted America

The greatest revival in modern history was begun in a little village which was formerly known as East Germany. It was a town called Herrnhut and led by Count Nicholas Von Zinzendorf. In 1727, a group of Moravians fled persecution in Czechoslovakia and immigrated to Germany. Zinzendorf allowed them to settle on his estate. They came and built a village they called Hernnhut which means - **"The Watch of the Lord"**.

Earlier in their history a prophet by the name of Malchoir Schaefer, gave a prophetic word that stated, **"God will place a light on these hills that will illumine the whole world."** This may appear to be impossible as a group of 300-400 people in a little village could birth such a word. These were refugees, kicked out of their own country and living in an obscure place in a backwater corner in Germany. Can you believe that God would do something here that would affect the world?

> **Point to Ponder:** "We must begin to believe that God, in the mystery of prayer, has entrusted us with a force that can move the Heavenly world, and can bring its power down to earth." - Andrew Murray

In 1722, Zinzendorf bought the Berthelsdorf estate from his grandmother and installed a Pietistic preacher in the local Lutheran church. That same year Zinzendorf came into contact with a Moravian preacher, Christian David, who informed the young Count of the sufferings of the persecuted Protestants in Moravia. These Moravians known as the Unitas Fratrum were the remains of John Huss' followers in Bohemia. Since the 1600s, these saints had suffered under the hands of successive repressive Catholic monarchs. Zinzendorf offered them asylum on his lands. Christian David returned to Bohemia and brought many to settle on Zinzendorf's estate, forming the community of Herrnhut (The Watch of the Lord). The community quickly grew to over three hundred. Yet due to divisions and tension in the infant community, Zinzendorf gave up his court position and became the leader of the brethren, instituting a new constitution for the community.

On August 13th, 1727, they went to a nearby village of Berthelsdorf to meet together in the Lutheran Church for a communion service. Count Zinzendorf got up to lead the service and got part way through **when the Spirit of God fell.** No one who was there ever gave a detailed description of what happened. They just said the fire of God fell, there were signs, wonders, and miracles, and they were never the same again.

Fire on the Altar

There was a new spirituality that characterized this community, with men and women being committed to encouraging one another in the life of God. August of 1727 is seen as the Moravian Pentecost. Zinzendorf said August 13th was *"a day of the outpourings of the Holy Spirit upon the congregation; it was its Pentecost."* The next week they said, *"How do we keep this going? God's presence is with us. How do we keep it?"* They turned in their Bibles and found that in Exodus 29: 41-43, God gave instructions and how to live in His presence! If you **keep the fire burning on the altar** (Exodus 29, Leviticus 6:13), I will dwell with you! They determined to keep the fire on the altar. They divided the clock into watches and took turns praying 24 hours a day 7 days a week! **Within two weeks of the outpouring, over twenty men and women covenanted to pray "hourly intercessions," thus praying every hour around the clock.** They were committed to see that *"The fire must be kept burning on the altar continuously; it must not go out"*.

Point to Ponder: "Don't pray when you feel like it. Have an appointment with the Lord and keep it. A man is powerful on his knees." - Corrie ten Boom

---

The numbers committed to this endeavor soon increased to around seventy from the community. This prayer meeting would go non-stop for over one hundred years and is seen by many as the spiritual power behind the impact the Moravians had on the world. The result was that the glory of God rested in their midst.

A Missionary Movement Born

The Spirit of God began to send them out as missionaries. In the 1700's missionaries went from there to Greenland, North and South America, South Africa, Australia, and even Tibet. They also went to England and one person that was saved there through their ministry was John Wesley. He met a Moravian Bishop Peter Bohler as they were crossing the Atlantic on a ship in the mid 1700's. They came upon a storm and the ship was being overwhelmed. The British passengers were in a panic state as they thought they were going to die. John Wesley was stunned by the calmness of the group of Moravians led by Bohler. These German Moravians were singing hymns and had this sense of peace. Wesley thought they were unaware of the storms severity and they were about to perish. He approached Peter Bohler and said we are about to die. Bohler responded by saying, *"We're not afraid to die. We die daily."* This impacted Wesley so much that he resolved to learn about these people. He went to Herrnhut and caught the **fire of the Lord** and brought revival to England.

> **Point to Ponder:** "God does nothing except in response to believing prayer." - John Wesley (Famous evangelist who spent 2 hours a day in prayer)

Wesley was a spark that led to the first Great Awakening. The nation was "transformed" and England was saved from a bloody revolution that France endured. The revival in England affected America. It was called "The Great Awakening" which transformed America as it swept through the colonies. Church attendance doubled in America. The U.S. Constitution was written, for most part, by men impacted by the "Great Awakening". The very foundations of our government were influenced by this prayer movement where people were faithful to take watches before the Lord and pray.

> **Point to Ponder:** "Whole days and weeks have I spent prostrate on the ground in silent or vocal prayer." - George Whitefield - (A great Evangelist during American Revolution era, during the first Great Awakening in America)

The missionary zeal from the prayer room at Herrnhut has hardly been surpassed in church history. The spark initially came from Zinzendorf's encounter in Denmark with Eskimos who had been converted by Lutherans. The Count returned to Herrnhut and conveyed his passion to see the Gospel go to the nations. As a result, many of the community went out into the world to preach the gospel, some even selling themselves into slavery in order to fulfill the great commission.

A simple statistic would best convey the impact that this prayer movement had upon the world. Normally, when it comes to world missions the Protestant laity to missionary ratio has been 5000:1. The Moravians however saw a much increased ratio of 60:1. By 1776, some 226 missionaries had been sent out from the community at Herrnhut. It is clear through the teaching of the so-called "Father of Modern Missions", William Carey, that the Moravians had a profound impact on him in regard to their zeal for missionary activity. The impact of this little community in Saxony which committed to seek the face of the Lord day and night has truly been immeasurable.

Point to Ponder: "If I could hear Christ praying for me in the next room, I would not fear a million enemies. Yet distance makes no difference. He is praying for me." - Robert Murray McCheyne

---

From this "Watch of the Lord" laborers went into the harvest field of the world. We need to impact our culture as never before. The Christian voice must resound and be heard loud and clear. There is no telling how many millions of souls were saved because of Herrnhut. They were a *radical remnant*! God will certainly intervene into man's affairs today in our nation if we seek Him wholeheartedly.

Can churches, ministries, and individuals come together today to take prayer watches? Yes. The **prayer closet** is a key as individuals must take personal time before the Lord. Can you commit to ½ hour a week or more? Why not take a daily watch in prayer at a designated time each day and seek the Lord? You can **declare the region you reside in will be the next Herrnhut** and a model to the nation.

Historical Cycle of a Nation - A Picture of America?

The average age of the world's greatest civilizations from the beginning of history has been about 200 years. This quote that comes from an unknown source is quite insightful:

"A democracy is always temporary in nature; it simply cannot exist as a permanent form of government. A democracy will continue to exist up until the time that voters discover that they can vote themselves generous gifts from the public treasury. From that moment on, the majority always votes for the candidates who

promise the most benefits from the public treasury, with the result that every democracy will finally collapse due to loose fiscal policy, which is always followed by a dictatorship."

As I read this quote above I certainly see that America is hanging in the balance. Study the present course of actions of our nation's government. Do you see any correlation with legislation and decisions our national leaders are presently making? There must be a return to a Biblical worldview!

Study this historical cycle below and look at the historical progression of a nation. It was attributed to a historian by the name of Alexander Tyler, but research revealed its authorship is unknown. I have added some new insights to it such as **degeneracy** and **moral depravity**. We must consider the spiritual perspective of why nations rise and fall. The Old Testament certainly reveals what brings the demise of a nation. This is the gauge we measure by. Only righteousness can exalt a nation as sin is a reproach to the people (Proverbs 14:34). **This is why we need a Herrnhut to manifest in America.** Do we have a choice if America is to be salvaged? Praying by a *radical remnant* will determine if we receive *revival or judgment.* I pray for a "great awakening" in America to come forth in Jesus name.

Where do you see America on this scale below?

(Every 200 years nations have progressed through the following sequence.)

1. Bondage and Severe Persecution – Result of selfishness and depravity.

2. Spiritual Faith – Vision, purpose and destiny birthed in a few.

3. Great Courage – People rise up and make a stand.

4. Liberty – Freedom comes from self-sacrifice and pursuit of truth.

5. Abundance – Blessings resulting from freedom.

6. Complacency and Apathy – Ease, comfort, affluence, distraction, lack of prayer.

7. Selfishness – People again turn to living for self, pleasure, and lusts.

8. Dependence – Work ethic is destroyed, welfare, and people live off of others.

9. Degeneracy and Moral Depravity – The flesh rules over spirit and sin abounds.

10. Bondage – The enemy of our souls brings captivity and judgment.

America is a land of the free where God has bestowed upon us great blessings and favor. This abundance had made us lose sight of God who is our provider, and we see ourselves turning to pleasures and lusts of the world. We are now becoming a dependent society where a developing moral depravity will cast us into bondage. The *radical remnant* and the prayer closet can turn this nation back. The model of Herrnhut is a hope we can look to.

Point to Ponder: In the long history of the world only a few generations have been granted the role of defending freedom. In the greatest hour of danger we are facing we have been handed an opportunity and a responsibility of unprecedented proportions. We are that generation. Now is the time! The question is who will rise up and learn from the historical model of Hernnhut? Day and night 24/7/365 prayer is the solution. Make this declaration over your nation, state, region or city and take the initiative and be part in raising up the greatest prayer movement America has ever experienced.

---

*"For in the **time of trouble He shall hide me** in His pavilion; in the secret place of His tabernacle He shall hide me; He shall set me high upon a rock."* **(Psalm 27:5)**

• 3 •

THE CHALLENGE – FACING REALITY!

We must be realistic. Most, if not all Christians, will acknowledge that prayer is vitally important. So what are the facts? Surveys indicate concentrated personal prayer time is very foreign to many who profess Christ as Savior. The stark reality is that very few take personal time to seek God and nurture a relationship with Him on a daily basis. The good news is that a praying *radical remnant* is awakening

*"And He said to them, "It is written, 'My **house** shall be called a **house of prayer**,' but you have made it a 'den of thieves.'"* (**Matthew 21:13**)

Point to Ponder: "When we calmly reflect upon the fact that the progress of our Lord's Kingdom is dependent upon prayer, it is sad to think that we give so little time to the holy exercise. Everything depends upon prayer, and yet we neglect it not only to our own spiritual hurt, but also to the delay and injury of our Lord's cause upon earth. The forces of good and evil are contending for the world. Had there been importunate, universal and continuous prayer by God's people, long ere this, the earth had been possessed for Christ." - E.M. Bounds.

Would you agree that prayer is of utmost importance and that we need to pray more? Agreement in thought, does not necessarily translate into action...especially when it comes to prayer. I am not saying people do not pray, but it is the **disciplined, committed personal prayer time** of which I am referring. As I have spoken in various locations on this subject, I find that people will nod in agreement with me. But the agreement falls short in making the decision to literally take time to pray at a predetermined specific time each day. Why are we not able to make time for the creator of all things?What is in the human spirit that stops us? Is the lack of prayer the result of a backslidden church? Seven days without prayer makes one **weak**.

Point to Ponder: "The battle of prayer is against two things in the earthly realm: wandering thoughts, and lack of intimacy with God's character as revealed in His word. Neither can be cured at once, but they can be cured by discipline." - Oswald Chambers

---

*"Watch and pray, lest you enter into temptation. The **spirit indeed is willing**, but the flesh is weak."* (**Matthew 26:41**)

Many of us understand the benefits and blessings that result from communion with God. We must be honest though and confess that there is still not enough praying. Do I see an awakening in this area? **I most certainly do**, so the challenge is to take advantage of the grace and time God is giving us.

As we see our nation at risk, deteriorating and eroding before our very eyes, with families being destroyed, it would seem that this would result in people crying out to God like never before. We are in a time of crisis. Also, there is a fear is at work that fuels our enemy's purposes. It is incapacitating to some and is being used to destroy our nation. The secret place is the place of safety that will remove all fears and restore hope. This book is meant to be **an encouragement and a call for people to go into their prayer closets or the secret place**, to communicate and nurture their relationship with God. I see that my own children and grandchildren's futures are at stake.

*"Though an army may encamp against me, **my heart shall not fear; **though war may rise against me, in this **I will be confident**."* (**Psalm 27:3**)

> **Point to Ponder:** "Little praying is a kind of make believe, a salve for the conscience, a farce and a delusion." E. M. Bounds

Am I hearing you right Lord in this challenge of personal and private prayer? Is the prayer closet or secret place the key to see a true transformation of society? What are we doing with the precious time God has granted each of us? Man's life is likened to vanity and like a shadow it passes away (Psalm 144:4). We are like a flower that fades and grass that withers (1 Peter 1:24). Let us put everything in perspective with the remaining breaths we have. We need God's guidance, direction, and protection. He is calling us to pray.

> **Point to Ponder:** "You may as soon find a living man that does not breathe, as a living Christian that does not pray." - Matthew Henry

"He who dwells in the secret place of the Most High shall abide under the shadow of the Almighty. I will say of the Lord, "He is my refuge and my fortress; My God, in Him I will trust.' Surely He shall deliver you from the snare of the fowler and from the perilous pestilence. He shall cover you with His feathers, and under His wings you shall take refuge; His truth shall be your shield and buckler. You shall not be afraid of the terror by night, nor of the arrow that flies by day, nor of the pestilence that walks in darkness, nor of the destruction that lays waste at noonday." **(Psalm 91: 1-6)**

Examining the Condition

Let us first discuss general corporate prayer meetings. Why would prayer meetings in general be the least attended of all functions that the church sponsors? If you would hold a dinner or a luncheon, attendance always seems to increase. Why is so little time relegated to prayer during a typical church service? Have church programs and schedules overridden the importance and power that resonates in prayer? **Prayer is not to be relegated to some side attachment in any church service.** Isn't it true that the sermon is the main feature in the majority of churches today?

> **Point to Ponder:** "There is no other activity in life so important as
> that of prayer. Every other activity depends upon prayer for its best
> efficiency." - M.E. Andross

In the late 19th century, the great orator, writer and pastor, Charles
Spurgeon, helped fuel a massive growth of Christianity in England
with his fiery brand of preaching, and his stirring and thought-
provoking essays and devotions. Operating out of the Metropoli-
tan Tabernacle in London, Spurgeon lead a congregation of more
than 10,000 people each Sunday in teaching, prayer and worship.
At the exact time he was preaching to the masses, members of his
church were in the Tabernacles boiler room holding a prayer vigil.
These early date prayer warriors were specifically asking for God's
blessing over the services led by Spurgeon. This unique approach to
prayer, no doubt played a large role in the success and effectiveness
of Spurgeon's ministry and the spread of Christianity throughout
19th-century Europe. *"One night alone in prayer,"* says Spurgeon,
*"might make us new men, changed from poverty of soul to spiritual
wealth, from trembling to triumphing."*

> **Point to Ponder:** "We are too busy to pray, and so we are too busy to
> have power. We have a great deal of activity, but we accomplish little;
> many services but few conversions; much machinery but few results."
> - R. A. Torrey

Many Questions – Think about it!

Are you convinced and believe that prayer does work? Does God
answer prayer? Will God meet all of our needs if we ask Him? Will
the presence of the Lord manifest if we seek Him? If the answers
were yes, the room would not be able to contain the size of the
crowd that would attend a prayer meeting. So what is the problem?
Is it a lack of faith, where individuals do not really believe prayer
works? Is it a lack of commitment? Are people walking in ignorance
regarding prayer? Is the church not being properly taught on prayer?
Do people lack desperation and a passion to pray? Could it be the

distractions and cares of the world are hindering people's private prayer times? Are people not interested in seeking God and His face to develop a personal intimate relationship? Do we lack a righteous standing with God that results in unanswered prayers? **Do we not recognize our position as priests before God?** Are we living independently from God instead of depending on Him for all of our needs? Do we really want to experience the presence of the Lord and His glory? How desperate are we? God will not do anything except in response to believing prayer.

*"The **righteous cry out**, and the **Lord hears**, and **delivers them** out of all their troubles. The Lord is near to those **who have a broken heart**, and saves such as have a **contrite spirit**."* **(Psalm 34: 17-18)**

Point to Ponder: "The one concern of the devil is to keep Christians from praying. He fears nothing from prayerless studies, prayerless work and prayerless religion. He laughs at our toil, mocks at our wisdom, but he trembles when we pray." - Samuel Chadwick

---

If you were told by the owner of a large department store that you could fill your shopping cart with whatever you need, would you show up at the appointed time? The only expense would be your time and commitment. What about if you were to receive an inheritance? All you had to do was show up at a particular time and sign the papers. The answer to these questions most likely would be yes. Are we not adopted children in the Kingdom of God?

*"And because **you are sons**, God has sent forth the Spirit of His Son into your hearts, crying out, "Abba, Father!" Therefore you are no longer a slave **but a son**, and if a son, then **an heir of God** through Christ."* **(Galatians 4: 6-7)**

We have received an inheritance because of what Jesus accomplished on the cross. We have been made priests and kings (Revelation 1: 5-6). The prayer closet is a place we can humbly lay claim to what has been given to us as children of God. We must make time to come before the throne of grace and communicate difficulties, issues, needs and then claim the inheritance.

*"Let us therefore come boldly to the throne of grace, that **we may obtain mercy and find grace to help in time of need.**"* (Hebrews 4:16)

Raising up the Apostolic

We hear today much about the word <u>Apostle</u> being used in the modern day church. This is one of the five fold ministry gifts. The main thrust of any true apostolic movement should be **to rally the people to pray.** The people must get up out of the pews. Apostolic leaders must rise up and encourage people to pray. These leaders, especially pastors, must be examples and set the pace. **Prayer will birth more prayer.** A praying pastor will beget a praying sheepfold. The greatest leaders in the church will be those who can inspire others to pray.

Point to Ponder: "The man who mobilizes the Christian church to pray will make the greatest contribution to world evangelization in history." - Andrew Murray

---

On what are you spending your time?

Time is one of our most valuable resources. Why not give a portion each day solely to the Lord who gave us eternal life? It is no excuse to say I have no time as we all have 24 hours in a day. We can and will make time for what we consider important. **The little importance we put on prayer is evidenced from the little time we give to it.** We have to ask ourselves what will be eternally fruitful. Why am I not taking time each day to seek the Lord, knowing full well someday I will see him face to face? Can we be part in making the region where we live the next Herrnhut?

Point to Ponder: When we face personal challenges it is at this time where many find it difficult to pray and seek God. One may feel overwhelmed and come under condemnation. They know they should pray but the pressure can overtake them. If you find yourself in this state cry out to God and begin disciplining yourself and making time. Breakthrough will come!

We will all stand before God and give an account for what we have done with our time, talents, and resources. As each day passes by we should carefully examine what we have done with our time. Will the Lord say "depart from me" or "well done my good and faithful servant"? We are all one heartbeat from eternity. I challenge you to declare that this is a new day where you will communicate with God in a new and fresh way. I truly believe that those who will be most revered by God are those who have done the most and best praying. The office of the church is to pray!

Point to Ponder: If you knew it was your last day on earth would you pray differently?

Make an Appointment

If you were interested in politics and the President of the United States contacted you and invited you to have a lunch date with him, would you clear out your schedule and make time? Let's say you are a biking enthusiast and Lance Armstrong contacted you or Lebron James, if you were a basketball fan. Would you make time in your schedule? What about some Hollywood celebrity or other famous individual? Do you get the point? **We will make time for what we consider important.** Jesus Christ the King of Kings is knocking at the door of your heart to fellowship and meet with you. What time will you give Him today?

"Behold, I stand at the door and knock. If anyone hears My voice and opens the door, I will come in to him and dine with him, and he with Me." **(Revelation 3:20)**

We have many examples in God's Word where men and women who sought the heart of God, through personal intimate prayer, found divine intervention. There are many heroes of the faith who walked the earth, and claimed their success was a result of personal prayer. Why have we not learned from their example?

Point to Ponder: The great reformer, Martin Luther, born in the late 1400s was once asked what his plans were for the following day, "Work, work, from early until late. In fact, I have so much to do that I shall spend the first three hours in prayer."

Dominion and Authority

"All the ends of the earth will remember and turn to the Lord, and all the families of the nations will bow down before him, for **dominion belongs to the Lord** *and he rules over the nations."* **(Psalm 22: 27-28)**

God is all powerful; He is the King and moral governor of the universe. Prayer is the way God interacts with man to affect His purpose here on earth. We each have been given stewardship over the land on which we walk, the resources put into our hands, and the gifts and talents God has given to us. We each have a harvest field where souls are at stake regarding eternity. It has been appointed for man once to die then the judgment (Hebrews 9:27). Eternity hangs in the balance and must be stamped on our eyeballs.

A CHALLENGE: Have you identified and written down all the names of those in your sphere of influence? Are you consistently praying for them? Have you written down exactly what you want to see accomplished in their lives? Do you believe we have this responsibility? What about praying for cities, universities or even nations of the world?

Point to Ponder: One day George Mueller began praying for five of his friends. After many months, one of them came to the Lord. Ten years later, two others were converted. It took 25 years before the fourth man was saved. Mueller persevered in prayer until his death for the fifth friend, and throughout those 52 years he never gave up hoping that he would accept Christ! His faith was rewarded, for soon after Mueller's funeral the last one was saved.

A Prayer Testimony

An African American student had stopped to chat with me after hearing me preach the Gospel in an open-air setting on a particular campus. His name was Mohammed and he was from the Detroit area. There was a stirring in his conscience regarding the present choices he was making. Raised in a Christian home, he said at one time he had faith in Jesus Christ as the only way, but now he was a Muslim and a follower of Islam. He indicated to me that his parents were praying for him. He kept questioning me regarding my thoughts and opinions on the Koran. I reviewed with him the very basics of the Christian faith. I saw he was troubled and stirred up inside, but he continued to defend Islam in many subsequent encounters. One day, I finally told him **I would like to pray for him.** I said my prayer would be that he would receive a direct encounter from God on what truth is - through a dream or vision - as I felt it was what he was truly seeking. I asked permission to put my hand on his shoulder. **He accepted and I prayed for him.**

The next week he came up to me and said that God had given him a dream. He asked my opinion on what it meant. He said he was in a room, instructing a bunch of students who were sitting on the floor in a circle. There was a thick, heavy door behind him with a small rectangular opening. A set of strange eyes peered through the opening looking at him. In his hands was a bag, and as he began to teach the students about Islam and the Muslim faith **he kept putting the Koran away and pulling out the Bible.** This happened repeatedly throughout the dream. I told Mohammed that the interpretation to me was rather simple: Jesus Christ and His Word were the only way, and God was trying to show him that he should put the Koran away and use the Bible as the only truth. As Mohammed walked away that day, I knew the Holy Spirit had touched him. He really wanted to know what the truth was, **and God was faithful and answered the prayer.**

*"The heaven, even the heavens, are the Lord's; But **the earth He has given to the children of men.**"* **(Psalm 115:16)**

Do we realize we have been given responsibility and access to God's unlimited power through the shed blood of Christ? We are responsible for the region we occupy and for the people within it.

The Gospel obtains its wings through prayer! Souls are at stake! Take your place and pray.

*"Moreover, as for me, far be it from me that **I should sin against the Lord in ceasing to pray for you**; but I will teach you the good and the right way."* (**1 Samuel 12:23**)

Point to Ponder: "Up in a little town in Maine, things were pretty dead some years ago. The churches were not accomplishing anything. There were a few Godly men in the churches, and they said: 'Here we are, only uneducated laymen; but something must be done in this town. Let us form a praying band. We will all center our prayers on one man. Who shall it be?' They picked out one of the hardest men in town, a hopeless drunkard, and centered all their prayers upon him. In a week, he was converted. They centered their prayers upon the next hardest man in town, and soon he was converted. Then they took up another and another, until within a year, two or three hundred were brought to God, and the fire spread out into all the surrounding country. Definite prayer for those in the prison house of sin is the need of the hour." - Dr. R.A. Torrey

---

Priests of the Lord

We have been made **priests and kings** because of what had been accomplished on the Cross. The difficulty, which has crippled the church, is that people in the pew do not recognize the power and responsibility they carry regarding a lost and dying world.

*"To Him who loved us and washed us from our sins in His own blood, and **has made us kings and priests** to His God and Father, to Him be glory and dominion forever and ever. Amen."* (**Revelation 1: 5-6**)

We are a holy priesthood (saved in Christ) that can stand in for those (sinners) who have no right standing with God. Wherever we walk we are ambassadors for Christ (2 Corinthians 5:18-21) and representatives of the most high God. We can bring before the throne of grace the unsaved and lost through our prayers (Hebrews 4:16). We are able to invade our culture through prayer. If we can grasp with our hearts and mind the power we have in prayer we will see transformation in our cities. Do you want to see a great awakening?

> **Point to Ponder:** He who runs from God in the morning will scarcely find Him the rest of the day. - John Bunyan

*"Coming to Him as to a living stone, rejected indeed by men, but chosen by God and precious, you also, as living stones, are being built up a spiritual house, **a holy priesthood, to offer up spiritual sacrifices** acceptable to God through Jesus Christ."* (**1 Peter 2:4-5**)

This is the personal challenge that we all face. Forget the past and start over. God will honor your decision to change. The secret place is the place where you will receive wisdom and understanding, where God will direct your steps (Psalm 37:23). This is the place of the *radical remnant*. If you are feeling any conviction after what you have read thus far, it is a good thing. This is the Holy Spirit bearing witness with your inner man. God is providing an opportunity for you to change direction and make a declaration: *"I will seek you with all my heart Lord"*. The past is the past and today is a new day. The sphere of influence that God has given you can be impacted by your prayers, and many souls will be won into the Kingdom. You are a priest and king of the highest God (Revelation 1: 5-6).

> **Point to Ponder:** "...the man on his knees has leverage underneath the mountain which can cast it into the sea, if necessary, and can force all earth and heaven to recognize the power there is in 'His name.'" - M.E. Andross

• 4 •

THE PRAYER CLOSET – DWELLING IN THE SECRET PLACE

What is the Prayer Closet?

"But you, when you pray, **go into your room, and when you have shut your door,** *pray to your Father* **who is in the secret place;** *and your Father who sees in secret will reward you openly."* (**Matthew 6:6**)

It is a place where we can go and be alone with God. It may be a designated room, a place where you walk in the woods or along the lakeshore, your car, even the rooftop, or any place where you can seclude yourself away from the busyness of the day. Isolation from distractions is a key element in finding your special place. You may have one particular place or a number of them. Just find a place to be alone with God. God is always ready to meet you. It is a secret place where you can talk to God out loud or communicate with Him in your thoughts. It is a place of self denial where we sacrifice our time; it is also a test of the sincerity and our devotion to God. You will be fed the bread of life in this place as you study the word of God (Luke 4:4).

The manna (bread of life) in the wilderness was only good for one day. The Israelites were told to gather fresh manna every morning (Exodus 16:12-31). Attempt to eat one meal a week and observe the physical toll on the human body. Give us this day our daily bread is an appeal within the Lord's Prayer (Matthew 6: 11). One of the primary purposes of the prayer closet is to be fed fresh manna daily to sustain our spiritual man. **When one is sick, loss of hunger is a symptom.** Is it possible that **not** seeking the Lord on a daily basis is a sign of spiritual sickness? Is the symptom the loss of spiritual hunger? Feeding solely on a Sunday morning sermon will leave us as spiritual skeletons.

*"Wait on the Lord; be of good courage, and **He shall strengthen your heart**; wait, I say, on the Lord!* **(Psalm 27:14)**

Point to Ponder: The word of God is the food by which prayer is nourished and made strong." - E. M. Bounds

---

The prayer closet is the place where you are spiritually nourished. It is a place where you privately communicate your innermost feelings, whether good or bad. You can be still and be silent and say nothing. **It is a place where you wait to hear God's voice.** It takes patience and faith to hear that small still inner voice speaking to you. It can be the place for you to cry out, declare, proclaim, make petitions, sing, praise Him and give thanks. Any of these actions are not uncommon in the closet of prayer – **that private and secret place**. The Lord's Prayer (Matthew 6: 9-13) may come into your mind, as it so beautifully breaks down the essential elements of a complete prayer. This secret chamber is literally the preserver of our relationship with God! It wonderfully clears the vision; steadies the nerves; defines duty; stiffens the purpose; sweetens and strengthens the spirit.

Point to Ponder: "He who has learned to pray has learned the greatest secret of a holy and happy life." - William Law

---

The prayer closet is a place of sanctification where you set yourself apart, giving quality time to the Lord where He can give you a moral cardiogram. The "lamp" of the Lord will search your heart (Proverbs 20:27). It is the place where Jesus the great physician can surgically remove (spiritually) the hindrances, setbacks, wounds, and issues of the heart. It is a place to examine your personal motives and intents of the heart (Hebrews 4:12) to determine why you do what you do. A spiritual inventory can be made where subtle areas of sin are exposed. This will create an environment of repentance that can be established daily. Let the Holy Spirit have its way!

*"Likewise the Spirit also helps in our weaknesses. For we do not know what we should pray for as we ought, **but the Spirit Himself makes intercession for us with groanings which cannot be uttered.** Now He who searches the hearts knows what the mind of the Spirit is, because He makes intercession for the saints according to the will of God."* **(Romans 8: 26-27)**

Remember, you are a priest of the Lord. Repentance and humility are catalyst that will restore intimacy with the Lord. This then leads to a relationship that will grow deeper. Love will be manifested as you set yourself apart in the secret place and you will feel the presence of the Lord if you are patient and do not give up. His living Word (Bible) will "set you apart" as you apply it in that secret place alone with God.

Point to Ponder: If people were taught how to pray while building a devotional life, counseling could be eliminated in the church. We are priests who can come before God in behalf of those who are not able - but also for ourselves (1 Peter 2: 4-5).

---

*"**Sanctify** them by your truth. Your word is truth."* **(John 17:17)**

*"For the **word of God is living and powerful**, and sharper than any two-edged sword, piercing even to the division of soul and spirit, and of joints and marrow, and **is a discerner of the thoughts and intents of the heart.**"* **(Hebrews 4:12).**

Jesus Christ is the word and truth (John 1:14, 14:6). In John 17 (the night before He died) Jesus was in a state of desperate prayer in the Garden of Gethsemane. The word Gethsemane means olive press. Jesus was squeezed in this place where the oil of the Holy Spirit was made available to us. He set Himself apart to be alone with God the Father. This time alone strengthened Him for what He was to endure on the cross. How much more do we need strengthening in these last days? We all have been called and given an assignment to fulfill a destiny here on earth. The prayer closet is the place where you will receive the blueprint and instructions to build and finish the task at hand.

*"For no other foundation can anyone lay than that which is laid, which is Jesus Christ. Now **if anyone builds on this foundation with gold, silver, precious stones, wood, hay, straw, each one's work will become clear;** for the Day will declare it, because it will be revealed by fire; and **the fire will test each one's work, of what sort it is.** If anyone's work which he has built on it endures, he will receive a reward. If anyone's work is burned, he will suffer loss; but he himself will be saved, yet so as through fire."* (**1 Corinthians 3: 11-15**)

Point to Ponder: "...True prayer is measured by weight, not by length. A single groan before God may have more fullness of prayer in it than a fine oration of great length." - C. H. Spurgeon

---

The prayer closet is the place where the Holy Spirit is allowed to touch the human spirit. The natural man cannot comprehend the things of God. We must allow the Holy Spirit to do its work in us and this takes place during times of intimate fellowship and communion with God. It is here where we have the mind of Christ! It is here where the *radical remnant* receives life.

*"But God has revealed them to us through His Spirit. For the Spirit searches all things, yes, the deep things of God. For what man knows the things of a man except the spirit of the man which is in him? **Even so no one knows the things of God except the Spirit of God.** Now we have received, not the spirit of the world, but the Spirit who is from God, that we might know the things that have been freely given to us by God. **These things we also speak, not in words which man's wisdom teaches but which the Holy Spirit teaches, comparing spiritual things with spiritual. But the natural man does not receive the things of the Spirit of God,** for they are foolishness to him; nor can he know them, because they are spiritually discerned. But he who is spiritual judges all things, yet he himself is rightly judged by no one. For "who has known the mind of the Lord that he may instruct Him?" **But we have the mind of Christ.**"* (**1 Corinthians 2: 11-16**)

> **Point to Ponder:** "The men who have done the most for God in this world have been early on their knees. He who fritters away the early morning, its opportunity and freshness, in other pursuits than seeking God will make poor headway seeking Him the rest of the day. If God is not first in our thoughts and efforts in the morning, He will be in the last place the remainder of the day." - E.M. Bounds

How Do I Establish an Effective Prayer Closet Time?

To establish an effective prayer closet time we must focus on the discipline and commitment involved. We must also recognize that there are definite needs where the only remedy comes through prayer. Prayer must be looked at as a **trade to be learned**. It may be very difficult and challenging to us as we pursue the Lord, but you must be encouraged to take one day at a time and learn. It will take much thought, practice, painstaking time, and labor to become skillful in a career you may be choosing. Prayer closet time of the *radical remnant* is no different. I can attest to this by personal experience.

> **Point to Ponder:** We are constantly bombarded with outside stimuli. We have been conditioned in the West to have short attention spans that rob us of the patience to wait and be still. We always want it fast and want it now. Press through what appears to be boredom thresholds.

Some individuals **are fearful of establishing a set prayer closet time** during the week because they see it as making a vow before the Lord. They feel that if they do not keep the appointment, God will act angrily and they will be condemned. This is a lie! God is love (1 John 4:8). We all will face situations where we are called out to take care of some task or commitment. Is it possible we could forget the time we established? Yes! God prefers mercy over judgment so never let anything deter you from setting a time. You are not under the letter of the law. It is the motive and intent of the heart that God sees.

Another common struggle when establishing a committed time is a feeling that may come over you where you may ask yourself - *what am I accomplishing?* There are times you may feel like a wagon stuck in the mud. You may not hear an answer right away. Do not fall into a neglect of spending time with God if this happens, but stay the course and press ahead to the high calling. There will be times when **God will speak to you at a different time than you are asking.** It could be driving down the road, shopping or maybe in the shower. God may speak to you about things that were not even on your mind. Just go with the flow as it is all part of the calling you have in Him. Develop a God consciousness. He can speak through a friend, movie, pictures, a billboard, dreams, and of course God's Word. Be alert, listen and watch.

*"No one who **puts his hand to the plow and looks back** is fit for service in the kingdom of God."* (**Luke 9:62**)

Point to Ponder: "I would rather teach one man to pray than ten men to preach." - Charles Spurgeon

---

Discipline: To instruct or educate; to inform the mind; to prepare by instructing in correct principles and habits; a method of regulating principles and practices.

Commitment: To give in trust; to put into the hands or power of another; to engage or make a pledge. It is a total giving of one's self over to something that one believes.

We easily make time for what we want to do. Establishing an effective prayer closet time is based on what we _**want to**_ do as opposed to what we feel we _**have to**_ do in regards to making prayer time. We must not look at prayer as a meaningless duty to perform or to be crowded into the busy part of the day. It should not be slipped in at the end of the day when we are tired. A _**want to**_ mentality must be sought where quality time is set aside. Your time in the prayer closet is an investment in eternity. This sowing of time will reap a life in the spirit. You may experience some discouragement at times to surface to test your commitment. Always remember when a seed is planted it takes time to grow.

Point to Ponder: "I suspect I have been allotting habitually too little time to religious exercise as private devotion, religious meditation, scripture reading, etc. Hence I am lean, cold, and hard. God would perhaps prosper me more in spiritual things if I were to be more diligent in using the means of grace. I had better allot more time, say two hours or an hour and a half, to religious exercises daily, and try whether by so doing I cannot preserve a frame of spirit more habitually devotional, a more lively sense of unseen things, a warmer love to God, and a greater degree of hunger and thirst after righteousness, a heart less prone to be soiled with worldly cares, designs, passions and apprehensions and a real undisassembled longing for heaven, its pleasures and its purity." - William Wilberforce

---

Love can manifest only from a heart that **_wants_ _to_** love and not out of some fear or force where we feel we **_have to_**. The scriptures encourage us to seek the Lord, wait on him, cry out, ask, knock, never give up, be still, rest in Him, and abide in His presence.

A Turning Point Teaching

In May of 2009, I listened to a teaching regarding spiritual burn out. Mike Bickle (IHOP - Kansas City) was teaching on how to avoid burnout or losing touch with God. The first area that we all need to tackle is disciplining ourselves. There has to be an inner strength where you say enough is enough, where you persevere in the setting of new goals. He had indicated that we must discipline ourselves on a daily basis to read God's Word, pray, as well as rest and soak in the Lord. Setting aside a disciplined time each day is a challenge in our modern day world, but is ultimately necessary to establish a close relationship with our Lord.

Point to Ponder: If you give a hungry person a fish to eat and satisfy his hunger, he will be full for one day. If you teach that person how to fish instead, he will never go hungry. Prayer will take care of all your needs in life – learn how to pray!

In the late 80's and early 90's I was disciplined to seek the Lord on a daily basis. I set aside and committed time each day. I could hear the Lord and feel his presence. The doors of ministry I had stepped through currently were a result of those prayers. **I then fell into a trap of being busy for the Lord, but not properly waiting on Him.** I would still pray each day, but there was no set time. I call it popcorn praying. After hearing this teaching by Mike Bickle the Holy Spirit convicted me to return to the place where God dwells. This I have done and this book is a result of that obedience to that still small voice. I believe I am hearing a message for the time and season we are presently in for the nation.

Do you have Oil for your Lamp?

Carefully read the parable of the 10 virgins (Matthew 25: 1-13). There were five who were wise and had oil for their lamps. There were also five virgins who were foolish and let their lamps go out. The prayer closet is the place to **receive the oil** so your **light can shine** and the **lamp will burn** so you can see. The Holy Spirit of God will meet you in that secret place and give you the oil and any reserve you need. **Ask for oil for your lamps.** This is the place to buy and sell. Keep your lamps filled as it will enable you to face all storms and challenges that lie ahead! Your lamp will shine even in the darkest of days. What is the cost? It is your time, commitment, and energy in the prayer closet. It will take your labor to enter into that place of rest. The reward is an intimate relationship with the Lord Jesus Christ. We need the oil of intimacy!

Stirrings in the Heart

Charles Finney, also known as America's greatest evangelist, said, *"When the outer revelation of truth bears witness with the inner revelation in our hearts, it is like the grinding of two millstones."* This results in conviction of the Holy Spirit. **Conviction presents a challenge to take action and be obedient by changing and making a decision to go in the opposite direction.** The right decision will please God and bring favor and blessing as His storehouse of promises is opened. If you feel that tugging on your heart to pray more - than be obedient.

*"Do not love the world or the things in the world. **If anyone loves the**

world, the love of the Father is not in him. *For all that is in the world, the lust of the flesh, the lust of the eyes, and the pride of life, is not of the Father but is of the world. And the world is passing away, and the lust of it;* **but he who does the will of God abides forever.**" **(1 John 2: 15-17)**

Making a decision to establish and **commit to a prayer closet time** is the first step. Prayer is the will of God, and it is the key to bringing divine intervention into the affairs of mankind. The discipline must come from an inner resolve that this is God's will and that you **want to** please Him.

Point to Ponder: "I have so fixed the habit in my mind that I never raise a glass of water to my lips without asking God's blessings, never see a letter without putting a word of prayer under the seal, never take a letter from the post without a brief sending of my thoughts heavenward, never change my classes in the lecture room without a minutes petition for the cadets who go out and for those who come in." Stonewall Jackson (Civil War General)

"You who hear prayer, to you all flesh will come." **(Psalm 65:2)**

One Step at a Time

The next step is to not fret and wonder what do I do during this personal prayer time that I had set aside. How do I pray? What do I pray? What do I say? How do I act? Is it being quiet or talking out loud? Do I stand, dance, sit, kneel, or lay prostrate? Do I just be still or do I need to pace back and forth? Can I listen to worship music and meditate on God? Should I study the Word of God? The answers to these questions are very simple yet hard for so many to grasp in order to pro-actively engage the Lord in the prayer closet. There is no set formula! All of the above mentioned actions are correct. Even though in my earlier walk with the Lord I understood the prayer closet, I was challenged by these questions above. It was like my mind needed to be renewed.

Point to Ponder: "The Word of God represents all the possibilities of God as at the disposal of true prayer." - A. T. Pierson

I also found and realized that the study of God's Word and prayer go together. Where we find one the other will be found. The study of God's word in the prayer closet must be heartfelt and not from the head. It is good to obtain insights and principles but the heart must be impacted. Many have head knowledge of God but do you really know Him in an intimate way? Approaching the word of God in a way where you are performing a **ritualistic duty** must be avoided. Come expecting to receive and encounter the Lord Jesus Christ. Sometimes you may find yourself reading the Bible and your mind will drift with little concentration. If this happens read the Bible out loud to yourself. You will find the focus return.

There will be times of quiet and resting in God where you block out all outside thoughts. There will be times you will cry out to God and make loud declarations or speak quietly and then be silent. You may sit, pace, lie down, or kneel. I have been in all of these positions when communicating with my wife. Why not with God? I am His bride by the way and God loves us. We are his children!

> **Point to Ponder:** D. L. Moody understood the importance of daily prayer. Each morning he would take personal prayer time by isolating himself in an old coal shed to be alone with God.

There will be times where we must **turn our lips into a set of ears** in order to listen. You may sing praises and give thanks and even dance before Him. David did (2 Samuel 6:14). The prayer closet can be a place of intimacy, a place of sorrow, where you cry out to God. Crying can be looked at as **liquid words** as tears can convey more than a spoken word. God will respond to tears (Psalm 56:8)! It is a resting place where we can be quiet and still. Hearing the voice of God is probably one of the most important benefits of this personal prayer time (Matthew 13:9). This quiet listening while being silent can open up many doors of opportunity. It can be a place where you birth something that God has revealed to you. It is a place of abiding and best of all, where you can enjoy His presence.

Point to Ponder: In the world of sports there is a place where all athletes like to be and that is **"The Zone"**. It is a mystery to sports psychologist. When an athlete enters this place he/she functions in complete excellence. The concentration is so pure that the performance is near perfect. Sports psychologists have found that the only things that disrupt this desired place are fear and anger. The prayer closet is the place where you can enter **"The Zone"**. The devil always attempts to provoke us into anger and make us fearful to disrupt prayer that will remove mountains. Remember that perfect love casts out all fears. Entering the **"Prayer Zone"** will remove the obstacles that hinder you in life.

Laboring to Rest

*"Come to Me, **all you who labor** and are heavy laden, and **I will give you rest**. Take My yoke upon you and learn from Me, for I am gentle and lowly in heart, and **you will find rest** for your souls. For My yoke is easy and My burden is light."* (**Matthew 11: 28-30**)

*"There remains therefore a rest to the people of God. For **he that is entered into his rest, he also hath ceased from his own works**, as God did from his. **Let us labor therefore to enter into that rest,** lest any man fall after the same example of unbelief."* (**Hebrews 4: 9-11**)

When I read the scripture above (KJV – Hebrews 4: 9-11) it appears to be an oxymoron. How could two opposites be true? How can labor result in rest? I have discovered that **it takes effort and diligence on my part to rest.** We must endeavor and have an earnestness to do it. There is so much distraction in the media centered and digital world in which we exist. We are so busy with demands on our life and then there is the stress! It can be a labor just to set time aside and seek God. Finding that place of stillness results in a peaceful rest where you cease from your own works and gain the confidence to accomplish what God has called you to do. It is His strength working in you.

Point to Ponder: The Lord said to rest one day of the week and cease from what we normally do the rest of the week (Sabbath day). The fourth commandment (Exodus 20:8) was not a suggestion but instead a commandment. Could the prayer closet be to us today as the Sabbath is to the week? It is the place where your spiritual batteries are charged, where productivity increases, and is a wellspring of life to face any challenge you may face.

"Wisdom is the principal thing; therefore get wisdom. And in all your getting, get understanding. Exalt her, and she will promote you; she will bring you honor, when you embrace her. She will place on your head an ornament of grace; a crown of glory she will deliver to you." **(Proverbs 4: 7-9)**

I have recently made it a practice to pray daily for:

1. Wisdom and Understanding
2. Revelation as I read the Word of God
3. Oil for my Spiritual Lamp to See and be Ready
4. To Enlarge the Capacity of my Heart to Hear His Voice
5. Grace to Fulfill my Calling and Destiny
6. To Abide in His Presence.

In my **laboring to rest** I have discovered that Jesus Christ is wisdom and understanding. Resting in Him allows me to experience His presence. His presence is what instills wisdom into me and where I can receive the oil of the Holy Spirit to guide my steps. Let us labor to be in Christ Jesus! It is He who can only build our spiritual house of prayer.

"Rest in the Lord, and wait patiently for Him; do not fret because of him who prospers in his way, because of the man who brings wicked schemes to pass." **(Psalm 37:7)**

Point to Ponder: Remember the Jabez prayer of 1 Chronicles 4:10 - *"And Jabez called on the God of Israel saying, "Oh, that You would **bless me** indeed, and **enlarge** my territory, that **Your hand would be with me,** and that You would **keep me** from evil, that I may not cause pain!" So God granted him what he requested."*

• 5 •

COMMUNICATION NURTURES RELATIONSHIP

Relationship is nurtured through communication. Jesus Christ (the Son) always took personal time to communicate with God (the Father). God the Father and the Son Jesus Christ are one. We are adopted sons and daughters and brought into the family of God and have a relationship through repentance, faith, and salvation. Jesus prayed in John 17 that we should be one together and one in God. After a relationship is established, it is through communication with God (prayer) that will develop and build it. Jesus, who was God in the flesh, was our example. The stronger **the relationship, the more favor and blessings** are available. God wants to know us as He calls us His friend. His Word is a love letter to mankind where God has revealed His heart.

God desires intimacy with us but we must do our part and pour out our innermost thoughts, frustrations, and feelings. Communication is a developmental process that takes time. Communication with God will remove the veils and blind spots in our life faster than anything else. It is because this close relationship with God always results in His loving care for His children. Many look at the cross as a place of pain and suffering but it is the place of absolute love.

Point to Ponder: While being still in the prayer closet, many times you will be inundated with outside thoughts that interrupt the fellowship you were trying to obtain. I suggest you take a notebook and write down those things that you need to do in order to stop them from repeatedly cropping up in the mind. Your notebook will also be the place to write down God given vision and plans that you may receive as you silently listen. A personal revelation may also be given.

Communication is the **key to any developing relationship**. It is here where one gets to know the person with whom you are communicating. It is in this place where love grows and develops. We will begin to understand the person with whom we are communicating. God so desires to reveal His attributes, His nature, and His character. Before I married my wife, I learned who she really was through communication. It was not just her outward attractive appearance, but I understood her heart. **Relationships built on outward appearance will eventually fail.** The more I got to know her, the more I wanted to be around her. I became jealous of her affections. It was through communication I knew I wanted to be with her the rest of my life. The relationship grew to a point where I would lay my life down for her. I was in love!

*"I love those who love me, and those who **seek me diligently** will find me."* **(Proverbs 8:17)**

God is no different. Jesus Christ broke the curse of the law (Galatians 3:13), and He sits at the right hand of the Father making intercession for us (Hebrews 7:25). We can walk with God as Adam and Eve did originally in the garden. We can establish a relationship with the Godhead through communication. God is so willing to respond, if we would only take time to speak with Him.

Point to Ponder: "The prayers of God's saints strengthen the unborn generation against the desolating waves of sin and evil. Woe to the generation of sons who find their censors empty of the rich incense of prayer; whose fathers have been too busy or to unbelieving to pray, and perils inexpressible and consequences untold are their unhappy heritage. Fortunate are they whose fathers and mothers have left them a wealthy patrimony of prayer." - E. M. Bounds

The prayer closet or secret place needs to be the primary focus of our Christian walk. I was inspired years ago by reading a prayer series by E. M. Bounds, a Civil War chaplain. It was at that time, the Lord was speaking to me to leave my employment to go preach the Gospel on university campuses. But remember, as we get busy in ministry, we must not neglect meeting with God privately in our prayer room. I can share this from experience! Yes, I would still pray daily, but many times in a hurried and scattered fashion. As I have prayed Proverbs 4:7 for wisdom and understanding God has shown me to return to the prayer closet. It is in the secret place – His chamber – where all the promises of God are set before us (Psalm 91:1-10). On May 4th, 2009 I made a decision to return to the prayer closet and to never cease returning regularly again to that place.

Point to Ponder: "Therefore, whether the desire for prayer is on you or not, get to your closet at the set time; shut yourself in with God; wait upon Him; seek His face; realize Him; pray." - R. F. Horton

---

Loving God in the Prayer Closet

What are the two greatest commandments? Is it possible the prayer closet could in part fulfill these two commandments? I sincerely believe that the prayer closet helps fulfill the command to love God and our fellow man.

*"Jesus said to him, 'You shall **love the Lord your God with all your heart,** with all your soul, and with all your mind.' This is the first and great commandment . And the second is like it: **'You shall love your neighbor as yourself.'"*** (Matthew 22: 37-39)

I have discovered, though, that the church has emphasized loving God quite adequately in word, **but there remains shallowness in the understanding and application of it.** It is one thing to say we love someone, but how do we show it? We can say we love God, but how do we express that love? The "prayer closet" is one place and a way to love God. A revelation of **"how to"** love must be better explained to young and old. As a Christian, this concept was rather vague to me. I then began to question if I was really loving God and others around me the way I should. I was striving for greater understanding on the actual heartfelt application of the word <u>love</u>. I discovered prayer is one of those applications!

> **Point to Ponder:** When you pray for someone it is one of the highest forms of love you can give to someone. It knits your heart to the one for whom you are praying. Since God loves mankind and He desires all to be saved, praying for others is showing love to God and knitting your heart to His desires.

I received a great revelation regarding the word *love* through a book written by Dr. Gary Chapman called *The Five Love Languages*. He shared insights on how there are five ways to love people. When you think about them, they all entail laying your life down, in some capacity, for others around you. I then applied them to God since we were made in His image (Genesis 1:26).

The Five Love Languages

Words of Affirmation – These are words spoken that give praise and thanksgiving. In the prayer closet we are able to magnify God for all that He has done. We are to give words of appreciation and recognize the small things as well as the big things God has done. These are life-giving words that build our own faith and confidence.

Acts of Service – Making a decision to enter the prayer closet is an act of service. It requires effort and sacrifice of your time. It is being a servant even when circumstances are not pleasant! The response that you make when you hear God's voice is an act of obedience and service.

Quality Time – It is giving God your undivided attention, focusing on and communicating with Him with no outside distractions, while setting aside a daily time to seek Him, and just being still. This time spent is honoring and loving God.

Giving Gifts – The significance of the gift is the thought behind it, and for the most part, it is your time before God in this case. Time is a gift you can give someone. This gift is the giving of ourselves. Present yourself as a living sacrifice with a willingness to lay your life down to the Lord. Time is one of our most valuable resources.

Physical Touch – It is a way of communicating emotional love with God the Father, Jesus Christ the Son, and the Holy Spirit. Physical touch is feeling the presence of God and where you sense His awareness. When you open yourself up to God He is touched and in turn He will touch you in mind, body, spirit and soul. The human flesh will respond to the touch of God.

> **Point to Ponder:** "Our prayer must not be self-centered. It must arise not only because we feel our own need as a burden that we lay upon God, but also because we are so bound up in love for our fellow men. We feel their need as acutely as our own. To make intercession for men is the most powerful and practical way in which we can express our love for them." - John Calvin

Adam and Eve in the Garden

Can you imagine yourself walking through the Garden of Eden and directly talking with God? We see before the fall that there was a direct two-way communication. Man was allowed to directly communicate with the creator of the universe. When Jesus Christ shed his blood and died on a cross and rose again, direct communication lines were opened. Even as I walk my own property in the woods of northern Michigan, I have to put everything into perspective and realize that **I can talk directly to God**. If Adam and Eve could do it, why couldn't I? Doesn't the shed blood of Jesus Christ allow me to come before his throne of grace boldly (Hebrews 4:16)? Hosea 4:6 says *"My people perish for lack of knowledge."* God says let us reason together (Isaiah 1:18). This is communication! So I am learning to talk with God. We will be tested in our perseverance and sincerity in any relationship we pursue - but continue to pursue it.

> **Point to Ponder:** The day you stop pursuing God is the day your relationship with Him will begin to crumble and deteriorate. The leaven of the world will overtake you.

As you continue to come before Him and speak with God, make sure you take time and quiet yourselves and listen. It is during these times where impressions, thoughts, and an inner voice that speaks to you, will become evident, and eventually you will recognize it. You must have faith and patience.

*"For the **eyes of the Lord run to and fro throughout the whole earth,** to show Himself strong on behalf of those whose heart is loyal to Him."* **(2 Chronicles 16:9)**

We Are the Bride of Christ

Marriage was designed for two to be one in the bonds of intimacy (Genesis 2:24). In a sense God has made a proposal to marry us as He calls us the bride. Jesus Christ is the bridegroom, who was God in the flesh (Ephesians 5: 22-33). This marriage relationship with the Godhead is established through faith in Jesus Christ, who came, died, and rose again to take away the sins of the world. Repentance or the turning away from sin also establishes this marriage relationship. In any family relationship, whether it is between husband and wife, parents and children, or between brothers and sisters, it all hinges on **our ability to communicate with one another.** When love is communicated through word or deed, relationships strengthen. The serpent in the garden broke the communication between God and man because of the fall to temptation (Genesis 3). Jesus Christ gave us back our direct access to God.

> **Point to Ponder:** Oliver Cromwell was a great military and political leader in England who believed in being much upon his knees. Looking on one occasion at the statues of famous men, he turned to a friend and said: "Make mine kneeling, for thus I came to glory." It is only when the whole heart is gripped with the passion of prayer that the life-giving fire descends, for none but the earnest man gets access to the ear of God."

The enemy of our souls is always at work attempting to break our relationship with God as well as with each other. Disciplining yourself in personal prayer closet time will thwart the distractions, cares of the world, discouragement, and unnecessary busyness that Satan and his agents would utilize to break your relationship with God. As I have learned to communicate with my own earthly wife my marriage has remained strong. So God desires you to communicate through prayer and to be still, in order to deepen your relationship with Him.

Point to Ponder: Have you ever engaged in a discussion where the other party seemed detached and disinterested? If I truly love my wife/husband I most certainly would need to take time to directly communicate. Lack of communication often results in a breakdown of marriages. If my wife is trying to speak to me and I am reading the newspaper, surfing the web, or watching television, the relevance and intimacy of the conversation would be lost. I would certainly desire eye to eye contact where we each listen to the words the other is speaking. We each have a need to be heard. Why would God be any different? Engage the Lord with your body, mind and soul.

"Be still, and know that I am God; I will be exalted among the nations, I will be exalted in the earth." **(Psalm 46:10)**

*"But **those who wait on the Lord** shall renew their strength; they shall mount up with wings like eagles, they shall run and not be weary, they shall walk and not faint."* **(Isaiah 40:31)**

Adam and Eve lost the line to direct communication because of disobedience. They partook and ate the forbidden fruit of the tree of knowledge of good and evil. This choice was an act that gave up their dependence on God. The choice was independent of God's will. They both were removed out of the garden and stepped into bondage, and a curse upon mankind resulted. Jesus Christ came to break the curse of the law (Galatians 3:13), and it is our **relationship with God through direct communication** which invokes the inheritance we have received by faith. God has commended His love towards us (Romans 5:8), while we were yet sinners, and we are able to communicate with Him.

> **Point to Ponder:** Lack of personal prayer time in the closet is a reflection of one's independence from God or lack of dependence upon Him. It is literally saying, *"I can do it myself apart from God's help. My time is better given over to things of the world."*

Relationship Results in Divine Intervention

Mr. Daniel Nash was one individual who was given over totally to prayer. He nurtured a relationship with God. In the battlefields of the spiritual world the true heroes - *radical remnant* - are often the unseen by the world. These are the ones often touched by heaven who briefed the rarefied air of the secret place of the most high. Daniel Nash understood what dependence on God was all about. Such a one was a partner to the much better known evangelist Charles Finney (America's Greatest Evangelist) during the Second Great Awakening.

Daniel Nash started as a preacher in upstate New York. His record there is singularly remarkable. At age 48 he decided to give himself totally to prayer for Finney's meetings. Nash would come quietly into towns three or four weeks in advance of a meeting, gather three or four other like-minded Christians with him, and in a rented room start praying and bringing heaven near. It is reported that in one town, all he could find was a stuffy, dark cellar, but that place was soon illumined with holy light as he made it the place of intercession.

> **Point to Ponder:** Intercession is the response to pain whether it is for the lost that are dying around you or those who are suffering in the body of Christ. Your cries of intercession are urgent petitions as you beseech the throne of God on the behalf of others. Intercession is the bearing of burdens for the ones you are praying for.

In another place Finney relates, *"When I got to town to start revival a lady contacted me who ran a boarding house."* She said, *"Brother Finney, do you know, a Father Nash? He and two other men have been at my boarding house for the last three days, but they haven't eaten a bite of food. I opened the door and peeped in at them, because I could hear them groaning, and I saw them down on their faces. They have been this way for three days, lying prostrate on the floor and groaning. I thought something awful must have happened to them. I was afraid to go in and I didn't know what to do. Would you please come and see about them?"*

"No it isn't necessary," I replied. *"They just have a spirit of travail in prayer."*

When the public meeting started, Father Nash would not usually attend, but kept praying in his closet for the convicting power of the Holy Spirit to fall on the crowd and melt their hearts. If opposition arose, Father Nash would pray all the harder.

Point to Ponder: It is all in our perspective. When we face giants that hinder the progress of God's Kingdom we must look through the eyes of David when he faced Goliath. David did not run in fear but his perspective was different. He saw it as, *"look at the big target I have to hit."* So it must be with the mountains or giants we face. With God nothing is impossible.

At one time a group of young men promised to break up the meetings if Finney continued. Nash was praying nearby and came out of the shadows to announce: *"Now mark me, young men! God will break your ranks in less than one week, either by converting some of you, or by sending some of you to hell. He will do this, certainly as the Lord is my God!"*

Finney thought his friend had lost his sense. But by next Tuesday morning, the leader of the group suddenly showed up, confessed his sinful attitude before Finney and accepted Christ. "What shall I do Mr. Finney?" he asked. I, Finney, told him, "Go back to your companions and tell them how Christ had changed his life." Before that week was out nearly all of the original group had come to Christ.

*"So I say to you, **ask, and it will be given to you; seek, and you will find;***

knock, and it will be opened to you. For everyone who asks receives, and he who seeks finds, and to him who knocks it will be opened." **(Luke 11: 9-10)**

Point to Ponder: Prayer is the real work while evangelism is the mopping up.

In 1826 both Finney and Nash were burnt in effigy. The enemy recognized the threat of Father Nash's prayers to their ways of wickedness. Shortly before Nash died in 1831 he wrote: *"I am now convinced, it is my duty and privilege, and the duty of every other Christian, to pray for as much of the Holy Spirit as came down on the day of Pentecost, and a great deal more. My body is in pain, but I am happy in my God. I have only just begun to understand what Jesus meant when he said, 'All things whatsoever you shall ask in prayer, believing, you shall receive.'"*

It is interesting to note that within four months of father Nash's death Finney left the evangelistic field to take a church in New York City. His prayer partner in taking the enemy by storm was gone. He whose prayer had been the strength of the campaigns was now in his eternal home, and the loss of power was felt.

Point to Ponder: "There is no power like that of prevailing prayer, of Abraham pleading for Sodom, Jacob wrestling in the stillness of the night, Moses standing in the breach, Hannah intoxicated with sorrow, David heartbroken with remorse and grief, Jesus in sweat of blood. Add to this list from the records of the church your personal observation and experience, and always there is the cost of passion unto blood. Such prayer prevails. It turns ordinary mortals into men of power. It brings power. It brings fire. It brings rain. It brings life. It brings God."
- Samuel Chadwick

• 6 •

GOD'S HOUSE IS A HOUSE OF PRAYER

Are We a Spiritual House?

Jesus said that His house (church) would be called a "House of Prayer" (Matthew 21:13). What is this house that He was referring to?

And He said to them, "It is written, 'My house shall be called a house of prayer,' but you have made it a 'den of thieves.'" (**Matthew 21:13**)

Was Jesus speaking of a church or a building? Was it a place where people would gather to pray? Or could it be referring to individuals who pray by themselves? The answer is yes to all of the above questions. A church or place where people gather to pray is a house of prayer. The greater revelation is **we each are individual houses of prayer** that can open heaven anywhere and anytime.

"For we are God's fellow workers; you are God's field, you are God's building." (**1 Corinthians 3:9**)

Individually, we are the Church as well as part of the corporate church body. **So churches can be a house of prayer as well as individuals who go into the prayer closets.** It can be where two or three are gathered in Christ's name, because He dwells in our midst (Matthew 18:20). You also have access to God's throne by an instant, direct wireless connection – your voice. We must conclude according to the Scriptures, we are individual walking houses of prayer with spiritual authority. When these houses of prayer and/ or lively stones come together corporately in prayer it is a powerful force that will impact the earth.

*"Coming to Him as to a living stone, rejected indeed by men, but chosen by God and precious, you also, **as living stones, are being built up a spiritual house**, a holy priesthood, to offer up spiritual sacrifices acceptable to God through Jesus Christ."* **(1 Peter 2: 4-5)**

Point to Ponder: When asked how much time he spent in prayer, English evangelist and philanthropist George Muller's reply was, "Hours every day. But I live in the spirit of prayer. I pray as I walk and when I lie down and when I arise. And the answers are always coming."

So again, are we a spiritual house and priests of God where Jesus has called forth to pray? Yes, the scriptures are plain, clear and simple. We are called a **building of God**, also **lively stones** comprising a corporate and personal spiritual house, as well as the **temple of God.**

*"Or do you not know **that your body is the temple of the Holy Spirit who is in you**, whom you have from God, and you are not your own? For you were bought at a price; therefore glorify God in your body and in your spirit, which are God's."* **(1 Corinthians 6: 19-20)**

We are individually the temple of God where the Holy Spirit dwells. We each have an individual foundation and cornerstone which is Jesus Christ (1 Corinthians 3:11, Ephesians 2:20). We each are called spiritual houses, kings, and priests (Revelation 1: 5-6) that can offer up spiritual sacrifices unto God.

Point to Ponder: "As is the business of tailors to make clothes and cobblers to make shoes, so it is the business of Christians to pray." - Martin Luther

Incense Burning on the Altar

The strength of any church will be determined by the people **who individually in their private time seek God.** They already come with God burning in their heart. An established connection with God is already up and running. When you lose your connection with God you lose your ability to fulfill your God-given call and destiny. Part of that call is to minister unto our Lord in prayer, offering up spiritual sacrifices.

*"To Him who loved us and washed us from our sins in His own blood, **and has made us kings and priests** to His God and Father, to Him be glory and dominion forever and ever. Amen."* **(Revelation 1: 5-6)**

God's Word calls us **priests** as well as **kings**. It took much effort to prepare the incense as we see in the Old Testament (Exodus 30: 34-38). There was much beating and blending that took place. Prayer is referred to as an incense going up to God filling the bowls in heaven. Only a worthy priesthood can open up the heavens. You are that priesthood!

Point to Ponder: How desperate are you? Have you ever seen a drowning man? He will do anything for his next breath of air. Have you seen one gripping onto a ledge as he is about to fall? His whole body is mustering all the strength it possibly can to climb up and survive. What individuals has God put into your sphere of influence? They need your prayers. You are able to come before God in their behalf on a daily basis.

---

*"Let **my prayer be set before you as incense**, the lifting up of my hands as the evening sacrifice."* **(Psalm 141:3)**

Every time we seek the Lord in our prayer closet, it is an opportunity to fill a bowl. When it spills over onto earth it gives wings to the Gospel. If we really desire to see signs, wonders, and miracles manifest, we must go back to the blueprint laid out by the Lord regarding prayer.

"Now when He had taken the scroll, the four living creatures and the twenty-four elders fell down before the Lamb, each having a harp, and **golden bowls full of incense, which are the prayers of the saints.***"* **(Revelation 5:8)**

Whether it's spiritual or physical incense, you need fire to make the fragrance rise and give it spirit and life. We must be earnest and lay hold of God, never giving up, until we receive the blessing. This type of **prayer closet time** that I am talking about is simple, but yet very hard. Make a choice and declare that I will be fervent, passionate, and seek the Lord with all of my mind, heart and soul. The priests of God must keep the fire on the altar burning (Exodus 29: 41-43, Leviticus 6:12). We are the modern day priest because of Christ who was after the order of Melchizedek (Hebrews 7:17).

Point to Ponder: Charles Finney was known as America's greatest evangelist. He once said, "I once knew a minister who had a revival 14 winters in succession. I did not know how to account for it till I saw one of his members get up in a prayer meeting and make a confession. *"Brothers, he said, I have been long in the habit of praying every Saturday night until after midnight for the descent of the Holy Ghost among us. And now, brethren (and he began to weep), I confess that I have neglected it for two or three weeks."* The secret was out. That minister had a praying Church.

• 7 •

PRACTICAL PRAYER
APPLICATIONS

Anytime spent alone with God is not wasted. Prayer changes our whole being, our surroundings and equips every Christian who wants to live a life that counts.Whoever would desire to have power for service must take time in the prayer closet. **Prayer is a dialogue and not a monologue!** You are communicating with the creator of the universe. Try to grasp that as you sit and be still.

Prayer is a spiritual law that cooperates with the mind of God. It is the acid test of devotion. Language is secondary in true prayer. God knows and understands every thought that you have. It is an attitude of spirit and mind where prayer can clothe itself in reality and power. It is our weakness leaning on omnipotence. **Prayer is the secret of power.** We all desire to see signs, wonders, and miracles of God being released. There is a price to pay to be one that carries the presence of God - the *radical remnant*. It is not works but instead a relational connection with God. Prayer is a union with God as well as a desire to possess God Himself, the source of life. It is not always asking but instead receiving Him who is the giver of the blessings. Prayer is living a life of fellowship with God.

Point to Ponder: "The great people of the earth today are the people who pray! I do not mean those who talk about prayer; or those who say they believe in prayer; or those who explain prayer; but I mean those who actually take the time to pray. If they say they do not have not time, it must be taken from something else. **That something else is important, very important and pressing, but still, less important and pressing than prayer.** There are people who put prayer first, and group the other items in life's schedule around and after prayer. These are the people today who are doing the most for God in winning souls, in solving problems, in awakening churches, in supplying both men and money for mission posts, in keeping fresh and strong their lives far off in sacrificial service on the foreign field, where the thickest fighting is going on, and in keeping the old earth sweet a little while longer." - S.D. Gordon

PRAYER APPLICATION #1

Establishing the Prayer Watch of the Lord in Your Church or Region

Any state, city, county or region can decide to make 24/7 prayer throughout the year a reality. It takes a dedicated persistent few with **initiative** and **purpose**. There has to be a sense of desperation where a realization manifests that divine intervention is necessary to cure the ills of society. Man does not have the solutions any longer so the throne of God must be approached. We must come before God in behalf of those who cannot. It begins with us as individuals. Select a time each day or during the week where you can sit and be still before God. Designate this time as your time with God alone - this is your watch time. Intercede and pursue the heart of God as you walk and talk with Him. This is the *radical remnant* secret place prayer closet time.

Point to Ponder: "The true church lives and moves and has its being in prayer." - Leonard Ravenhill

Enlist Others to Pray

As you seek the Lord ask for direction on how you are to proceed to help increase prayer in your sphere of influence. Write the vision down (Habakkuk 2:1-4). **Begin to enlist people to take ½ hour, hour or 2 hour watches in prayer, praise, reading the Bible, devotions and worship whether on a daily or weekly basis.** This is what is called networking. It can be done in your church or region you live in. If you enlist or encourage only one person to participate you have done a very good thing. If you are a pastor or ministry leader you can activate a whole group of people!

*"Again I say to you that **if two of you agree on earth concerning anything that they ask**, it will be done for them by My Father in heaven. For where **two or three are gathered together** in My name, I am there in the midst of them."* **(Matthew 18: 19-20)**

Start a website if you are able to post times that people are willing to give you. It is an incremental step process. Be patient and do not give up. God will provide those of like mind if you ask Him. There is the praying *radical remnant* all around you waiting to be encouraged and released. You can be that fire starter.

SEE: www.TransformMI.com as a model.

PRAYER APPLICATION #2

Pastor Initiated 24/7 Prayer in the Local Church Body

What if a pastor or ministry leader recognized the importance of prayer? What if he/she saw that the days we are in needs a long term prescription of prayer to cure societal ills? If there is a stirring in you as you read this then please proceed as it is the Holy Spirit prompting you. The pastors are gatekeepers of the region they occupy. They allow what goes in and out of a city.

Point to Ponder: If the church wants a better pastor, it only needs to pray for the one it has.

Pastors and ministry leaders have been given a sphere of influence to shepherd. What if a church could select one day per week or one day a month where the congregation would be encouraged to pray? **The pastor could preach a series of messages on prayer.** He could appoint trusted individuals in his church to set up ½ to 2 hour prayer watches. A time schedule would be set up. People could volunteer to select times. This could be done by individuals, married couples, or even small groups. The prayer does not necessarily have to be at the church, but in the various homes and locations people select. A prayer guide could be developed where all areas of importance are covered (even local church issues). Would this further the vision of the local pastor? Yes! Would this strengthen the local church body? Yes!

NOTE: A word of encouragement should be given here to pastors and ministry leaders. Do not give up! Many times the spiritual pulse of a church is revealed by how many respond to your call to pray. You may find disappointment rise up as only a few people you are leading respond. Turn this into an opportunity to enlighten your sphere of influence regarding prayer and pray for them and not criticize or condemn. God will act in your behalf and stir them up. Be persistent!

Have you heard of Spurgeon's **"Boiler room"**? Five young college students were spending a Sunday in London, so they went to hear the famed C.H. Spurgeon preach. While waiting for the doors to open, the students were greeted by a man who asked, *"Gentlemen, let me show you around. Would you like to see the heating plant of this church?"* They were not particularly interested, for it was a hot day in July. But they didn't want to offend the stranger, so they consented. The young men were taken down a stairway, a door was quietly opened, and their guide whispered, *"This is our heating plant."* Surprised, the students saw 700 people bowed in prayer, seeking a blessing on the service that was soon to begin in the auditorium above. Softly closing the door, the gentleman then introduced himself. It was none other than Charles Spurgeon.

Point to Ponder: "Prayer is buried, and lost and Heaven weeps. If all prayed the wicked would flee from our midst." - Evan Roberts

If the church is a larger one of 300 people or more they could commit to a 24 hour period. A smaller church could select a 12 hour time period. If churches would work together in any locality, city, county or region transformation will occur. It begins with one church in a region who understands the importance of prayer.

"Rejoice always, **pray without ceasing,** *in everything give thanks; for this is the will of God in Christ Jesus for you."* **(1 Thessalonians 5:16-18)**

In this process churches must be allowed to keep their own identity. This is unity in our diversity. Churches must be allowed to pray as they are accustomed to. A true John 17 unity would manifest. Let's be visionaries and believe this could happen in the region we live. What if this took place in an entire state - county by county?

Point to Ponder: "Prayer is the greatest of all forces, because it honors God and brings him into active aid." - E.M. Bounds

---

PRAYER APPLICATION #3

Ten Minute Daily Prayer for the Nation

Is our nation's future presently at stake? Make a point to pray 10 minutes a day for your nation. It can be in your prayer closet or during your watch of the Lord. Utilize your car as you travel. You can be praying as you shop, taking a walk or on a bike ride. This is a daily spontaneous prayer with no set time if you wish. We all can carve out time each day as we each have 24 hours in a day. You have an instant wireless connection with God. All you have to do is lift your voice or pray quietly in your mind. God hears and will honor this time of communicating with him in behalf of our nation. It's not that prayer changes the purpose of God but it does change the action of God.

Point to Ponder: "There has never been a spiritual awakening in any country or locality that did not begin in united prayer." - A.T. Pierson

---

*"Confess your trespasses to one another, and pray for one another, that you may be healed. The **effective, fervent prayer of a righteous man avails much**. Elijah was a man with a nature like ours, and he prayed earnestly that it would not rain; and it did not rain on the land for three years and six months. And he prayed again, and the heaven gave rain, and the earth produced its fruit."* (James 5: 16-18)

PRAYER APPLICATION #4

Priesthood Breastplate Prayer – Bishop Larry Jackson

Bishop Larry Jackson (www.betheloic.com) once a keynote Promise Keeper speaker has initiated what is being called **"breastplate prayer"**. This prayer application will revolutionize the church and transform any city or region. We are all priests of God if we have repented of our sins and have faith in Jesus Christ (Revelation 1: 5-6). What we must realize as New Testament believers is that **the priesthood has changed but not the order of approach.** The shed blood of Christ is what allows you to come before Him.

The Old Testament priest wore a breastplate with 12 precious stones representing the 12 tribes (Exodus 28:21, 29, 39:14). There were four rows of three stones and the priests would stand in the gap for the nation of Israel before God. Initially, God desired the whole nation to be a kingdom of priests. Each stone represented a tribe in Israel. Why not place 12 people on your spiritual breastplate and **pray for these 12 individuals daily.** The **top row** would be for unsaved family members, the **second row** of three would be for friends and acquaintances, the **third row** for those in the workplace or neighborhood where you live and the **fourth row** for people you would never meet or encounter. This could revolutionize a church if all attending would take up this practice. This initiative would transform a city, county or a state if numerous churches participated across any region. What if every church took this prayer strategy to heart? Every person in the nation would be covered in prayer.

Point to Ponder: There has to be a major change on how we do church in the 21st century. There are principles in the first century church that must be applied. The body of Christ must be trained how to effectively advance the kingdom of God. We are the new priesthood - with authority! All great soul winners have been men and women of much and mighty prayer.

*"Now therefore, **if you will indeed obey My voice and keep My covenant,** then you shall be a special treasure to Me above all people; for all the earth is Mine. **And you shall be to Me a kingdom of priests and a holy nation.'** These are the words which you shall speak to the children of Israel."* **(Exodus.19:5-6)**

The Israelites **failed to obey God** after they said they would, so God appointed the Levites as the priesthood so they could stand for every individual. Aaron, his sons (Exodus 27:21) and the Levites were the priests (Deuteronomy 7:19) who could only come before God for the people (Numbers 3: 6-10).

*"And the Lord said to Moses, "Go, get down! **For your people whom you brought out of the land of Egypt have corrupted themselves.** They have turned aside quickly out of the way which I commanded them. They have made themselves a molded calf, and worshiped it and sacrificed to it, and said, 'This is your god, O Israel, that brought you out of the land of Egypt!'" And the Lord said to Moses, "**I have seen this people, and indeed it is a stiff-necked people!** (Exodus 32: 7-9)*

Point to Ponder: Adam was really the first priest of God as he walked daily and had fellowship with God in the garden. Adam had the right to come before God. He was given dominion over all of the earth (Genesis 2:28) and Adam had to dress, protect and keep the garden (Genesis 2:15). Part of that assignment was to worship God as He inhabits our praises. The word dress also meant to worship God. When the serpent came and Adam fell this fellowship was broken. Adam failed to protect the garden (Genesis 3). Today we have the opportunity as priests to fellowship with God, but have the same responsibilities as Adam. We have each been given a garden to cultivate and take care of each day - your area and sphere of influence.

Jesus Christ changed the priesthood (Psalm 119:4). Jesus Christ is that new priest after the order of Melchizedek. All who are born again through Jesus Christ have been made priests of God. Jesus sits on the throne at the right hand of God in heaven interceding for us. The people in the pews have been misrepresented as laity and a special clergy class has formed. **The people in the church must be released in their priestly duties to bring up before God daily those people that were placed in their sphere of influence.** We all share in the responsibility as being New Testament priests. There is no longer a special class of priests as Jesus changed the law.

"If perfection could have been attained through the Levitical priesthood (for on the basis of it the law was given to the people), **why was there still need for another priest to come - one in the order of Melchizedek, not in the order of Aaron?** *For when there is a change of the priesthood, there must also be a change of the law."* **(Hebrews 11: 7-12)**

Where are the **New Testament priests** to be released today in the highways and byways of society? The **cultural gateways** (Seven Mountains) in society must be impacted by this army of priests who are to offer up spiritual sacrifices (our prayers and labor in the Lord - Isaiah 2:2). This army must engage the family, church, governmental, educational, business, media, and entertainment realms. We are Gods priesthood today!

Point to Ponder: "Prayer breaks all bars, dissolves all chains, opens all prisons, and widens all straits by which God's saints have been held." - E. M. Bounds

---

"And they shall rebuild the old ruins, they shall raise up the former desolations, and they shall repair the ruined cities, the desolations of many generations. Strangers shall stand and feed your flocks, and the sons of the foreigner shall be your plowmen and your vinedressers. **But you shall be named the priests of the Lord, they shall call you the servants of our God.** (Isaiah 61: 4-6)

"Coming to Him as to a living stone, rejected indeed by men, but chosen by God and precious, you also, as living stones, are being built up a spiritual house, **a holy priesthood, to offer up spiritual sacrifices** *acceptable to God through Jesus Christ."* **(1 Peter 2: 4-5)**

What are these spiritual sacrifices? Prayer for the lost that God has put in your path. **Again, place 12 people on your <u>spiritual</u> <u>breastplate</u> and pray for these 12 individuals daily.** Do not tell them. When one gets saved you put another individual on your breastplate in his/her place. Your rewards are in heaven. This does not mean you are not to pray for others but instead are targeting these 12 and filling a bowl in heaven with your prayers. Be patient! Ask God and He will reveal to you assigned individuals that you will specifically pray for.

Point to Ponder: "Eighteen-year-old Hudson Taylor wandered into his father's library and read a gospel tract. He couldn't shake off its message. Finally, falling to his knees, he accepted Christ as his Savior. Later, his mother, who had been away returned home. When Hudson told her the good news, she said, "I already know. Ten days ago, the very date on which you tell me you read that tract, I spent the entire afternoon in prayer for you until the Lord assured me that my wayward son had been brought into the fold." He became the famous missionary to China and founder of China Inland Mission which birthed over 800 missionaries.

Revolutionizing the Church

This could revolutionize a church if all attending would take up this practice as you are a **<u>Priest of the Lord</u>** (1 Peter 2:4-5, Revelation 1:5-6). Breastplate prayer could transform a church, city, county or a state. **A church of 100 would now be a church of 1200** as you stand individually for the 12 on your breastplate. You are bringing them to church with you. The pews of the church will be released in a new sense of prayer for the lost. The church will have regained its authority through pro-active prayer as we are kings!

Point to Ponder: "... [the] power of prayer can never be overrated. They who cannot serve God by preaching need not regret. If a man can but pray he can do anything. He who knows how to overcome with God in prayer has Heaven and earth at his disposal." - Charles H. Spurgeon

---

"To Him who loved us and washed us from our sins in His own blood, and

has made us kings and priests to His God and Father, to Him be glory and dominion forever and ever." (**Revelation 1:5-6**)

As you **praise and worship the Lord on a Sunday morning,** visualize these people's faces in your mind and lift them up to the Lord to be saved. The pastor could take time for breastplate prayer during the service. **This prayer strategy will activate the church.** It will nurture church growth and result in more evangelism. Individuals in any church body will be given a meaningful purpose they can engage in as well as a sense of fulfillment. If churches across America could adopt this every soul in the nation would possibly be covered in prayer.

> **Point to Ponder:** "God's cause is committed to men; God commits Himself to men. Praying men are the vice-regents of God; they do His work and carry out His plans." - E.M. Bounds

Breastplate City Taking Prayer

Why not **select 12 cities** and lift them up before the Lord on your breastplate on a daily basis? It would begin with your <u>own</u> <u>city</u> and other important ones in your state and nation as well. **Why not pray for the peace of Jerusalem?** God will give you a burden for particular cities. See what the Lord can do through your persistent prayers. **Why not 12 university campuses?** Desperate prayer is what touches the heart of God and moves His hand. The *radical remnant* must be rallied to rise up and take their rightful place.

America needs desperate prayer! Where there is no vision of eternity there is no prayer for the perishing. The secret of all failure is our failure of secret prayer. What cities do you feel a burden for? This is your territory to occupy. God has entrusted each of us - the *radical remnant* - with the possibility of bringing the Kingdom of Heaven to earth with all of its power.

> **Point to Ponder:** "We are too busy to pray, and so we are too busy to have power. We have a great deal of activity, but we accomplish little;

many services but few conversions; much machinery but few results."
- R. A. Torrey

PRAYER APPLICATION #5

8PM Prayer Challenge

The number eight Biblically means "<u>new</u> <u>beginnings</u>". What if individuals across any region, state or nation would **start praying at 8:00pm every day for cities?** You could pray over your city and select others that are significant in your state. The prayer could last a minute, ten minutes, or an hour. The key is to have <u>one</u> <u>voice</u> rise up in one collective spontaneous sound that would resonate and ripple across the land. A corporate unity amongst denominations would manifest. This voice would shake the wilderness and bring divine intervention. **Individuals could put a candle in their window** that will symbolically show they are a house of prayer for cities in that state. Can you see windows across your state light up as a sign that this is a house of prayer?

*"And from the days of John the Baptist until now the kingdom of heaven suffers violence, and the **violent take it by force**."* **(Matthew 11:12)**

God gave us the kingdom and He gave us keys to the kingdom when Jesus died on the cross 2000 years ago. All that we have to do is open what God has given to us. Nothing can stop us now as we can take the kingdom to the world by force. Consider asking pastors, church, and ministry leaders to communicate this message out to their spheres of influence. Let us move out and began to pray, praise, declare and worship the King of Kings – Jesus Christ. We will let our lights shine and pray with passionate desperation. We will **pray with importunity** and bombard heaven with our prayers so the wilderness will be shaken.

*"I will declare the decree: The Lord has said to Me, 'You are My Son, Today I have begotten You. **Ask of Me, and I will give you the nations for your inheritance,** and the ends of the earth for your possession. You shall break them with a rod of iron; you shall dash them to pieces like a potter's vessel.'"* **(Psalm 2: 7-9)**

PERSONAL PRIESTHOOD
BREASTPLATE OF PRAYER

(Bishop Larry Jackson –
See **www.Betheloic.com** for in depth teaching.)

TOP ROW OF THREE STONES

*Select and pray for 3 unsaved family members.

1._____ 2. _____ 3. _____

SECOND ROW OF THREE STONES

*Select and pray for 3 friends or acquaintances.

1._____ 2. _____ 3. _____

THIRD ROW OF THREE STONES:

*Select and pray for 3 individuals in the workplace or neighborhood where you live.

1._____ 2. _____ 3. _____

FOURTH ROW OF THREE STONES:

*Select and pray for 3 individuals you would never meet or encounter.

1._____ 2. _____ 3. _____

NOTE: Copy this page and fill in and place it in your Bible as a reminder!

PRAYER APPLICATION #6

Seven Mountain Cultural Gateway Church Prayer Mobilization

Each church has individuals who are gifted and have great potential to further the kingdom of God. They are waiting to be encouraged to be released. Studies have shown that only 10-15% of people in the pew know their individual calling. What if each pastor could see their congregation as priests of God that could occupy and take an area they are sent out to engage on a daily basis. The pastors and church leaders have to recognize the opportunities we have available to us.

There is no better place to start **than with prayer.** We have referred to the seven mountains or cultural gateways in this publication a number of times. Each church body has people who are interested **in the family, church, education, government, business, media, and entertainment realms.** What if a pastor could divide the church into groupings according to occupation or areas of interest? Let's take teachers and educators for example. Develop a small group based on interest in education that would pray together for that cultural gateway. As new people would come into the church they could be directed into that group. Even those who did not have employment could be connected into a small group based on a particular interest. **The focus is prayer and building relationships through this process.**

> **Point to Ponder:** "Four things let us ever keep in mind: God hears prayer, God heeds prayer, God answers prayer, and God delivers by prayer." - E. M. Bounds

PRAYER APPLICATION #7

Neighborhood Prayer Invasion

Each church is surrounded by a community that they were called to impact with the Gospel of the Lord Jesus Christ. Begin to dedicate, declare and proclaim the neighborhood that surrounds your church is the Lord's. Invite Jesus Christ into that neighborhood and send out teams to walk and pray. Bless empty storefronts and existing businesses. As you walk or drive by homes God will reveal to you insights on how to pray. This can be called "drive by" prayers or prayer walking. You could target areas such as a business, drug house or any establishment of ill repute and intercede for individuals and the owners. We must bless and not curse. Blessing will bring the desired results.

You may directly encounter people so ask God to open up a door of utterance (Ephesians 6:19) to share the Gospel. Claim a 10 city block area and see what God can do. A pastor could assign members of the congregation to take on various neighborhoods. This is a pro-active strategy to engage the church to further the Kingdom of God. In time evangelistic teams could go door to door asking families what they specifically need prayer for. Opportunities will arise to share the Gospel. Invite people to church or a Bible study in this process. Prayer is the foundation for success. This is what the *radical remnant* has been called to do.

PRAYER APPLICATION #8

The Communion Table of the Lord*

How many people take Holy Communion on a daily or weekly basis? Many see it and have turned it into a monthly ritual at church. We must consider making this part of our prayer closet time. **Fellowship with God is available at the communion table.** As a priest of God you are able to administer and partake of communion as often as you wish.

Point to Ponder: "If you want that splendid power in prayer, you must remain in loving, living, lasting, conscious, practical, abiding union with the Lord Jesus Christ." - C. H. Spurgeon

---

*"For as often as you **eat this bread and drink this cup, you proclaim the Lord's death till He comes. Examine yourself** therefore whoever eats this bread or drinks this cup of the Lord in an unworthy manner will be guilty*

*of the body and blood of the Lord. But **let a man examine himself,** and so let him eat of the bread and drink of the cup. **For he who eats and drinks in an unworthy manner eats and drinks judgment to himself, not discerning the Lord's body. For this reason many are weak and sick among you, and many sleep. For if we would judge ourselves, we would not be judged.** But when we are judged, we are chastened by the Lord, that we may not be condemned with the world."* (**1 Corinthians 11: 26-32**)

It is a time to examine ourselves and to receive from the Holy Spirit. The promises of God are available **as there is healing in the communion table.** It is a time to remember what Jesus Christ accomplished on the cross and develop a greater sense of awareness and appreciation. This can be a time to invite the presence of God into your midst as you are safe in this secret place.

So consider taking daily personal communion utilizing the elements (Grape juice and Matzos). **The broken body (bread) breaks all oppressions and the blood (juice) takes away the sins of the world.** Declare the blood of the lamb over your home, neighborhood, city, state and nation.

Point to Ponder: "Closet communion needs time for the revelation of God's presence. It is vain to say, 'I have too much work to do to find time.' You must find time or forfeit blessing. **God knows how to save for you the time you sacredly keep for communion with Him.**" - A. T. Pierson

---

PRAYER APPLICATION #9

Civil Servant Prayer

How many times have we passed by a police car, a fire truck, an ambulance or an EMT vehicle? What about driving by a hospital where the sick and dying are with doctors and nurses trying to save lives? We have our military men and women who we know are presently serving in the armed forces. There are CERT and disaster personnel that need to be ready if a disaster strikes. What am I trying to say? Pray for a blessing of safety and wisdom for these people as they may be called upon to help you or one of your loved ones. Prayer is powerful and you may save the life of one being transported to a hospital as they pass by you with blinking lights and sirens. All of these little things add up to make you - the *radical remnant* - an effective praying servant of Christ.

Some have initiated adopt-a-cop programs where law enforcement is prayed for. This could be done for the mayor, city council, firemen and those who serve us in the civil arena. It takes one with the calling, heart and vision to make it happen in your community.

PRAYER APPLICATION #10

Calling the Men to Prayer

The men were always called out to war in the Old Testament. Prayer is modern day warfare. Our enemies are spiritual so we must inspire the men in the church to pray.

"For we do not wrestle against flesh and blood, **but against principalities, against powers, against the rulers of the darkness** *of this age,* **against spiritual hosts of wickedness in the heavenly places."** **(Ephesians 6:12)**

A pastor friend of mine began to impart this strategy in his church before the service. He called the men up in front of the congregation and they would pray 15 minutes before the service. The pastor led the prayer so as not to put anyone on the spot. This not only encouraged the women in the church, but also changed the atmosphere of the service for that morning. Little things can amount to big things. This pastor decided that his church would be a house of prayer.

PRAYER APPLICATION #11

Call of the Shofars

"Praise the LORD! Praise God in His sanctuary; Praise Him in His mighty firmament! Praise Him for His mighty acts; Praise Him according to His excellent greatness! **Praise Him with the sound of the trumpet;** *Praise Him with the lute and harp! Praise Him with the timbrel and dance; Praise Him with stringed instruments and flutes! Praise Him with loud cymbals;*

Praise Him with clashing cymbals! Let everything that has breath praise the LORD. Praise the LORD!" **(Psalm 150: 1-6)**

"Sing to the LORD with the harp With the harp and the sound [BLAST] of a psalm, **With trumpets [SHOFAR]** *and the sound of a horn; Shout joyfully before the LORD, the King."* **(Psalm 98: 5-7)**

I had to take time to mention a very <u>specialized</u> type of ministry where some consider it to work side by side with prayer. The Shofar is designed to break down spiritual walls and the bondages that hold people captive. It sends confusion into the enemies camp. The word horn always denotes power in the Bible. The Shofar is the first mentioned musical instrument in the Bible in praising of our God. In the N.T. it is called a trumpet.

THE SHOFAR IS: It is like a voice and it is not a man made instrument.

1. A Cry of War – Alarm for Battle
2. Instrument of Worship
3. Calling of the Intercessors - Congregation
4. Confusing the Enemy
5. Movement of the Camp

"When I **blow the trumpet,** *I and all who are with me, then you also blow the trumpets on every side of the whole camp, and say,* **'The sword of the LORD** *and of Gideon! Then the three companies blew the trumpets and broke the pitchers -- they held the torches in their left hands and the trumpets in their right hands for blowing -- and they cried, "The sword of the LORD and of Gideon!"* **(Judges 7: 18-20)**

"For the Lord Himself will descend from heaven with a shout, with the voice of an archangel, and **with the trumpet of God.** *And the dead in Christ will rise first."* **(1 Thessalonians 4:16)**

NOTE: What if intercessors and those who sounded Shofars surrounded a Mosque, a university, city hall, a state capitol or other area of importance? Could the atmosphere be changed in that place because of that sound of prayer and the blowing of the trumphet?

PRAYER APPLICATION #12

Houses of Prayer and Healing Rooms

What I am about to share is not new to many. There is a growing movement where neutral facilities are set up to open its doors to pray specifically for particular needs. They are being set up in regions of many states. For example, **why not establish a governmental house of prayer near each state capitol?** This location would function and focus on the prayer needs regarding government. Legislators as well as pending legislation could be prayed for. These types of houses of prayer would be set up where all denominations are respected in the way they choose to pray. There would be unity in our diversity. They are not designed to set up another church and must be run by individuals who are under authority of some pastor. They are not to compete with the local church but only be an arm of it.

Each state has areas that need to be addressed. Maybe a house of prayer could be established for every university. What about the Muslim community? In the state of Michigan there is a high concentration of Muslims in Dearborn and Southeast Detroit. There is a house of prayer being established with the primary focus to see Muslims saved in Jesus Christ. Every city or region could establish one for their city. The challenge is to work together and not allow jealousy, control or competition destroy the true purpose.

Healing rooms are also developing across the country in various localities. We have many sick amongst us - even in the church. Many Christians believe that it is God's will to heal. The Lord's prayer indicates how His kingdom is to come to earth. There is no sickness in heaven so why not bring heaven and healing to earth. As you Google healing rooms on the internet there are organizations that can help you in this effort.

• 8 •

THE HARVEST IS ALL AROUND US – PRAY!

We must not allow prayer to become a secondary tier in regards to our church services. It is prayer that births revival, renewal, transformation, and sends laborers into the mission field of life. **You cannot walk against the fall of man with the strength of the fall of man!** Studies have shown that the average pastor prays 3-5 minutes per day. If this is true we must help free up the time of these men and women of God. These gatekeepers must have direct access to the voice of God. It is through their inspiration where the people they shepherd can be encouraged to seek the face of God.

Point to Ponder: "Ministers who do not spend two hours a day in prayer are not worth a dime a dozen - degrees or no degrees." - Leonard Ravenhill

---

We need God's strength as well as anointing to bring His divine intervention into the sphere of influence where we have been called. This only manifests through prayer and a relationship with God. What is that mission field of life you have been called to? What is your mission field of life that you walk in? What is your mission field of life that you must pro-actively engage?

*"Then He said to them, "The harvest truly is great, **but the laborers are***

few; therefore **pray the Lord of the harvest to send out laborers into His harvest.**" **(Luke 10:2)**

"*No one who* **puts his hand to the plow and looks back** *is fit for service in the kingdom of God.*" **(Luke 9:62)**

Today the harvest field in many circles is popularly called the seven mountains or the seven cultural gateways. Bill Bright (Campus Crusade) and Loren Cunningham (YWAM) were simultaneously given by way of revelation the "Seven Mountains" that we in the church need to impact. Lance Wallnau (www.lancelearning.com), a brilliant Bible teacher, has popularized this very poignant teaching in what these men saw. Prayer is a central part of that pro-active strategy to engage our culture to bring God's intervention into our affairs.

Point to Ponder: Six per cent of our culture is shaped from the top down. This can be referred to as the "remnant elite". A few will make a big difference. Scale the mountain and take your place. You are created to be history makers as priests of the highest God. **Enlist to be one of the radical remnant elite that scales the mountain from the bottom to the top with desperate prayer.**

The Seven Mountains

"*Now it shall come to pass in the latter days that* **the mountain of the Lord's house shall be established on the top of the mountains,** *and shall be exalted above the hills; and all nations shall flow to it.*" **(Isaiah 2:2)**

In 1975, Bill Bright, founder of Campus Crusade, and Loren Cunningham, founder of Youth with a Mission, had lunch together. God simultaneously gave each of them a message to give to the other. This is what the message encompassed as described by Loren Cunningham.

"*The culture is shaped by seven mind molders, or mountains, in society. If we can influence each of these areas for Christ, we will win the culture of our nation. The Bible tells us that in the last days there will be sheep and goat nations. Sheep nations represent those who follow Christ; goat nations represent those who follow other* gods. *"All the nations will be gathered before Him, and He will separate them one from another, as a shepherd divides his sheep from the goats (Matthew 25:32)."* Who controls the seven mountains in a nation will determine whether that nation will be a sheep or goat nation.

In the book of Joshua, God calls Joshua to cross the Jordan River and to take the Promised Land. However, in order to do that, he had to drive out seven enemies that were more powerful than the people of Israel at the time. "This is how you will know that the living God is among you, and that he will certainly drive out 7 enemies before you including the Canaanites, Hittites, Hivites, Perizzites, Girgashites, Amorites, and the Jebusites (Joshua 3:10)." There were seven distinct enemies. They were to be driven out of the land. They were the rulers of seven mountains. Today, Christians have given these seven strategic mountains over to a liberal and secular leadership. God is calling his people to reclaim these mountains for His purposes (Loren Cunningham, founder of Youth with a Mission).

Point to Ponder: Jesus and Satan met at the top of a mountain and he (Satan) offered Christ the kingdoms of the world (7 Mountains). Whoever controls the kingdoms rules the world. Jesus took authority and spoke the Word. We can now bring the Kingdom of God to earth (Matthew 4). Prayer sends laborers into the mountains so His kingdom will manifest here on earth as it is in heaven. Prayer unlocks the doors to the world's kingdoms so scale the mountain God has put you on, choose to be part of the *radical remnant* praying elite.

This is a word by word transcript from Loren Cunningham regarding the seven mountains, or mind molders that shape any society or culture. He also describes his encounter with Bill Bright of Campus Crusade.

It was August, 1975. My family and I were up in a little cabin in Colorado. And the Lord had given me that day a list of things I had never thought about before. He said, "This is the way to reach America and nations for God. And (He said), "You have to see them *like classrooms, or like places that were already there, and go into them with those who are already working in those areas." And I call them "mind molders" or "spheres." I got the word "spheres" from 2 Corinthians 10, where Paul speaks in the New American Standard about the "spheres" he had been called into. And with these spheres, there were seven of them, and I'll get to those in a moment. But it was a little later that day, the ranger came up, and he said, "There is a phone call for you back at the ranger's station." So I went back down, about seven miles, and took the call. It was a mutual friend who said, "Bill Bright and Vonnette are in Colorado at the same time you are. Would you and Darlene come over and meet with them? They would love to meet with you." So we flew over to Boulder on a private plane of a friend of ours. And as we came in and greeted each other, (we were friends for quite a while), and I was reaching for my yellow paper that I had written on the day before, and he said, "Loren, I want to show you what God has shown me!" And it was virtually the same list that God had given me the day before. **Three weeks later, my wife Darlene had seen Dr. Francis Shaffer on TV and he had the same list! And so I realized that this was for the body of Christ.***

I explained my encounter for the first time in Hamburg, Germany at the big cathedral there to a group of hundreds of young people that had gathered at that time. And I said, "These are the areas that you can go into as missionaries. Here they are: Number one is the institution set up by God first, the family." After the family was church, or the people of God. The third was the area of school, or education. The fourth was media, public communication in all forms, printed and electronic. The fifth was what I call "celebration," the arts, entertainment, and sports, where you celebrate within a culture. The sixth would be the whole area of the economy, which starts with innovations in science and technology, productivity, sales, and service. The whole area we often call business, but we leave out sometimes the scientific part, which actually raises the wealth of the world. Anything new, like making sand into chips for a microchip, that increases wealth in the world. And then of course sales and service helps to spread the wealth. And so the last was the area of government. Now government, the Bible shows in Isaiah 33:22 that there are three branches of government, so it's all of the three branches: judicial, legislative, and executive. And then there are subgroups under all of those seven groups. And there are literally thousands upon thousands of subgroups. But those seven can be considered like Caleb: "Give me this mountain," and they can be a "mountain" to achieve for God.

Or they can be a classroom that you're going to disciple a nation in. Because Jesus said, "Go and disciple all nations." And it also can affect us, because in those areas we can be changed, transformed by the Holy Spirit to be effective missionaries into the area that God has called us into, and we will see it as not just a job to get money to stay alive, but "as the Father sent Me, so send I you," Jesus said. Therefore, we can be missionaries, where the word "missionary" means "one sent" and one sent of Jesus. If you're a lawyer in a legal office, you are sent of God, you're sent to be his missionary, or if you're in Hollywood, or you're working as a dentist, or you're working as a doctor, everything you can do for the glory of God. You may be in the area of foodservices. The Bible says in Zachariah 14:20 that even the cooking pots will be called "holy" to the Lord. That's foodservices. Regarding transportation, everything from a bus driver to an airplane pilot or to a car dealer or whatever it is, it says even the veils of horses will be called holy to the Lord.So we make whatever we do, if we do it as unto the Lord, a sanctified, or a holy work, it is holy unto the Lord. It's not just the pulpit on Sunday, that's one of the spheres. It's also all the other spheres together, and that's how we achieve advancing the kingdom of God.

The seven areas (mountains) that need laborers (Luke 10:2) can be defined as the (1) church, (2) family, (3) field of education, (4) the world of government and law, (5) the corporate business world – which encompasses the economy, (6) arts and entertainment, (7) and finally media and communications. Whatever area you occupy or are part of is your mission field. Jesus said to occupy (Luke 19:13) or take hold of the sphere of influence given to you before He returns.

Fire up the Mountain

Have you ever seen a fire that begins at the base of the mountain? The fire will consume all in its path up the mountain. This is the idea of the *radical remnant* praying elite. Which of the seven mountains do you feel a passion to engage with heartfelt prayer? You can be the few that can turn back many. This prayer will enable those placed at the top of the mountain to better advance the kingdom of God.

Point to Ponder: We must never forget that personal prayer closet time does not negate our responsibility of pro-actively engaging the culture we live in. You are to be a laborer in the harvest. Seek the Lord for your assignment and destiny. Which of the seven mountains are you to impact? You are an ambassador for Christ in your sphere of influence (2 Corinthians 5:20). You are part of God's greater plan on the mountain He has placed you on.

Can you picture Christian educators and parents in a church or a region coming together to pray for schools? What about government to pray at a designated location? These are the fire starters that will send fire up the mountain.

Change the Format

In most church settings, prayer has been replaced by program, tradition, and formalities. It can be a show where the people in the pew are not mobilized but instead entertained. Time is structured and scheduled, so people are not inconvenienced. Prayer is generally brought forth with little desperation, fervency, and passion. It is no little wonder we find our nation in such desperate need. Why hasn't the church taken the "seven mountains" when the Word of God says we can move mountains? It is the lack of effective, fervent, and passionate prayer.

*"Confess your trespasses to one another, and pray for one another, that you may be healed. **The effective, fervent prayer of a righteous man avails much.**"* **(James 5:16)**

> **Point to Ponder:** "Since the days of Pentecost, has the whole church ever put aside every other work and waited upon Him for ten days, that the Spirit's power might be manifested? We give too much attention to method and machinery and resources, and too little to the source of power." - Hudson Taylor

We see Jacob wrestling all-night with the angel, never letting go which resulted in the favor of God with angels ascending and descending from the throne (Gen 32: 24-26). It is this commitment and passion that moves the hand of God."

*"Then Jacob was left alone; and a Man **wrestled with him** until the breaking of day. Now when He saw that He did not prevail against him, He touched the socket of his hip; and the socket of Jacob's hip was out of joint as He wrestled with him. And He said, "Let Me go, for the day breaks. But he said, "I will not let You go unless You bless me!"* (Genesis 32: 24-26)

What about Moses who interceded for his nation (Numbers 21:7)? We see Hannah crying out for a son and the Lord blessed her with Samuel (1 Samuel 1). Daniel prayed 3 times daily alone with God and received a revelation of the end times and was set free (Daniel 6:10). What about Elijah, David, the Apostle Paul, and our greatest example of desperate prayer – Jesus Christ? They were passionate and desperate for the hand of God to move. **They were a worthy priesthood that brought down God's manifest reign on earth.** They were living sacrifices.

*"I beseech you therefore, brethren, by the mercies of God, that you **present your bodies a living sacrifice**, holy, acceptable to God, **which is your reasonable service**. And do not be conformed to this world, but be transformed by the renewing of your mind, that you may prove what is that good and acceptable and perfect will of God."* (Romans 12: 1-2)

We are called God's building and must give Him permission to inhabit us. We have been given a free will to choose to accept or reject an opportunity to develop a relationship with Jesus Christ. That same free will must be used to choose to pray and seek God. We are to individually offer prayer as incense to fill bowls in heaven.

Can you imagine individuals praying daily in unity 24 hours a day, seven days a week, and 365 days a year in one accord? **This type of intensity in prayer will bring divine intervention** and transformation to anyplace. We are a nation at risk. Will you join the call and take your place to pray? Will you be part of that *radical remnant*? The **prayer closet** is the key.

Point to Ponder: "Satan trembles when he sees the weakest Christian on his knees." - William Cowper

---

"Even then I will bring to My holy mountain, and make them joyful in My house of prayer. Their burnt offerings and their sacrifices will be accepted on My altar; for My house shall be called a house of prayer for all nations." (Isaiah 56:7)

The realization must set in that **we are individually walking houses of prayer.** We have been given responsibility to stand in the gap for the sphere of influence we each had been given by God. Through faith and repentance we have become adopted children of God, who have obtained an inheritance. God's grace, coinciding with this inheritance enables us to become history makers.

Point to Ponder: Lack of proper prayer is the locust that devours the church and any nation as well. Do you see the locusts eating the very fabric of life in America? What will you do? It is time to pray to rid our nation of the locusts that are on the land.

The Wireless Network

Through a series of prophetic words, strong impressions, dreams, and physical signs, I was shown we have a wireless connection with God (24 hours a day – 7 days a week). This connection with God is like using our cell phones where we can call Him up and communicate anytime. The good news is there are no **"dead zones"** and we have a **3G network - the Godhead** (Father, Son, and Holy Spirit). We create our own dead zones by **not communicating with God.**

Lack of faith, disobedience, not fearing the Lord, little desperation or passion also create dead zones. The 3G network is always there for you as God is omnipresent. You have **"friends and family"** in your network on earth that you can stand in the gap for and connect to God through your prayers. Verizon bought out Alltel so we must **"tell all"** about the authority we carry in the Lord.

> **Point to Ponder:** The 4G network is now upon us. The Biblical definition of the number four means ruling and reigning over the world. It includes things in heaven and on earth. Prayer is the pathway to make this dominion possible.

The wireless connection God is giving you is instant and quicker than a call on your cell phone, any e-mail communication, tweet,or text message. The **prayer closet or secret place** is where you can connect to God instantly when you are in relationship with Him. This is a place where you are alone with God. He is your access point for all your provision and it is the place where all the divine supplies are stored. God will be your shelter and protect you - *the radical remnant.* Nothing will be able to withstand our God!

"He who dwells in the secret place of the Most High shall abide under the shadow of the Almighty. I will say of the Lord, "He is my refuge and my fortress; my God, in Him I will trust." Surely He shall deliver you from the snare of the fowler and from the perilous pestilence. He shall cover you with His feathers, and under His wings you shall take refuge; His truth shall be your shield and buckler. You shall not be afraid of the terror by night, nor of the arrow that flies by day, nor of the pestilence that walks in darkness, nor of the destruction that lays waste at noonday." **(Psalm 91:1-6)**

As we carefully listen to the Lord in the secret place or prayer closet, God will order and direct our steps (Proverbs 20:24). As we are aligned under Christ properly, there will be no interference, static or dropped calls. There is instant help as we face the trials of life.

> **Point to Ponder:** Make time to pray. "The great freight and passenger trains are never too busy to stop for fuel. No matter how congested

the yards may be, no matter how crowded the schedules are, no matter how many things demand the attention of the trainmen, those trains always stop for fuel." - M.E. Andross

A Personal Dream with a Directive Purpose

I was given a dream that a respected worship leader had about me. I thought at the time it was for that present time of ministry and moved ahead to apply it to the current situation I was in at that time in 2004. But it was for the future which really is the now - 2009-15. It was again showing me the importance of the prayer closet, hearing from the Lord His instructions, and moving in obedience to His directions.

THE DREAM – A CALL TO PRAY

NOTE: This dream was submitted to me by a friend (Jeff) who is an anointed worship leader. I have interpreted portions of this dream which I believe is a call to secret place prayer.

I (Jeff) was in a large community or village (not a city) and I (Jeff) was starving and hungry for food. There were thousands more like myself, going from house to house and store to store looking for food, but finding none. I should point out that the village was kind of like a frontier town, except that it was in the middle of the woods or forest.

After searching in vain for food for a while, a large number of covered army trucks came driving in, and I knew they had food. The trucks were covered 6 by 6's. I'm pretty sure they had a white star on the trucks and they were dark green.

Point to Ponder: Many of you reading this have been given a sign or a guidepost through a dream or some word spoken over you. Never take them lightly but pray for insight on what has been given. Revisit those signs and declare them over your circumstances.

Once the convoy of army trucks came into the village, the dream switched to a different scene. Now, I (Jeff) was on an upstairs level inside a large building. There were hundreds of other people in the room in front of me. They were all facing away from me and were looking at something deeper into the room. Everyone was standing still, and no one talked. In my mind, I knew that they were starving like me, and wanted food. So I walked among them and asked what they were doing and they pointed at you (Rick - author of this publication).

I then walked out of the crowd, and up to you (Rick). You were sitting with your legs dangling off a ledge that was very high off of the bottom level of the building. In my mind, I knew the ledge was high enough that if someone fell off, they would likely die. At the bottom level I could see tons of people milling around. I assumed that they were looking for food to. You had a __wireless phone__ (prayer – connection to God) in your left hand and you were having a conversation. Your right hand (authority from the Lord) was stretched out to block off a small (approximately 2 foot wide ledge) that extended to an opening in the wall (prayer closet), and I knew that it was where the army trucks were going to pass out food (God's provision as a result of prayer).

I (Jeff) think I may have touched your (Rick) shoulder, but either way; I got your attention and ask what was going on. You look very concerned and said, "This is very important, we need to wait on the Lord." You said it a second time, while gesturing and pointing with your right hand, "It's very important, that we all wait." Then you put the phone that was cupped to your ear and kept talking, and again blocked off the small ledge with your right hand.

I (Jeff) went back to the mass of people and told them what you (Rick) said, and they nodded in agreement and kept staring at you. No one talked or moved, we all just watched you as you kept talking, and we waited. That was the end of the dream.

NOTE: The opening at the end of the 2 foot ledge in the diagram is the prayer closet!

The phone is a picture of the personal direct connection we have with God. It is that secret place prayer that brings all the provision that is necessary. Jeff (who had the dream) is a gifted worship leader. It will be the prayer, worship, and waiting on God which will release His promises.

We must all enter one by one into the prayer closet (door in the picture) to receive the provision of the Lord. The hunger, obedience and <u>waiting on the Lord</u> will bring His intervention. It will take prayer, praise, and worship in a sense of desperation that starving people experience to move the hand of God. The prayer closet is the unique place where God will meet your needs especially in times of trouble.

Point to Ponder: When prayer has become secondary, or incidental, it has lost its power. Those who are conspicuously men of prayer are those who use prayer as they use food, or air, or light, or money." - M.E. Andross

---

Can America be Saved?

The Lord is calling His church to 24/7/365 day and night prayer. We are married to the Lord and each individual must recognize the responsibility we have as part of the wedding vows of which we have taken. Day and night desperate prayer is what will save our nation! A network of prayer can be established in each town, city, region and state where individuals will seek the Lord in their **personal prayer closets**. It will take God's grace and a move of the Holy Spirit to accomplish such an enormous task.

*"You shall no longer **be termed Forsaken, nor shall your land any more be termed Desolate**; But you shall be called Hephzibah, and your land Beulah; or the Lord delights in you, **and your land shall be married**. For as a young man marries a virgin, so shall your sons marry you; and as the bridegroom rejoices over the bride, so shall your God rejoice over you. **I have set watchmen on your walls, O Jerusalem; they shall never hold their peace day or night** you who make mention of the Lord, **do not keep silent, and give Him no rest** till He establishes and till He makes Jerusalem a praise in the earth."* **(Isaiah 62: 4-7)**

Point to Ponder: "My chief reasons for a day of secret prayer are that the state of public affairs is very critical and calls for earnest deprecation of the divine displeasure. My station in life is a very difficult one, wherein I am at a loss to know how to act. Direction, therefore, should be specially sought from time to time. I have been graciously supported in difficult situations of a public nature. I have gone out and returned home in safety and found a kind reception has attended me. I would humbly hope, too, that what I am now doing is a proof that God has not withdrawn his Holy Spirit from me. I am covered with mercies." - William Wilberforce

The Challenge

Individuals much step forward and commit to designated prayer times on a weekly (daily) basis (See Chapter 7). Can God turn the heart of a king? What about the president of a nation - Proverbs 21:1? Will righteousness exalt a nation (Proverbs 14:34)? Can we pray for angelic visitations, dreams, and visions for national leaders? Man's authority to rule comes from God and His hand can be moved in our behalf.

*"The **king's heart is in the hand of the Lord,** like the rivers of water; He turns it wherever He wishes."* **(Proverbs 21:1)**

Point to Ponder: Can America be the next Herrnhutt? Why can't we today initiate a prayer movement in our nation that will surpass all others? Who will rise up in our homes, churches, cities, counties, and states in America? Can 5 states in our nation rise up in 24/7 prayer and bringing forth a "tipping point" (See Chapter 12) so a nation can turn to God? Answer the call as our nation is hanging in the balance.

Can your Region be the next Herrnhut?

Remember the greatest revival in modern history was begun in a little village in a region that was formerly East Germany. In Chapter Two the story was given and explained how this revival impacted America during the "Great Awakening." Ask yourself, why not the state I reside in? Why not the county, state, nation, or region I live in? Nothing is impossible with God! The highest offices in the land can be impacted by day and night prayer. Are we not called to pray for those in authority? The only "change" we need is Godly change in our nation. The prayer closet and crying out to the Lord for mercy is the only way judgments can be turned back or lessened. The *radical remnant* will come forth in Jesus name!

"Therefore I exhort first of all that supplications, prayers, intercessions, and giving of thanks be made for all men, for kings and all who are in authority, that we may lead a quiet and peaceable life in all godliness and reverence. For this is good and acceptable in the sight of God our Savior, who desires all men to be saved and to come to the knowledge of the truth. For there is one God and one Mediator between God and men, the Man Christ Jesus." **(1 Timothy 2: 1-5)**

Point to Ponder: Smith Wigglesworth: "Intercession will unlock any safe in the world."

The Importance of Declaration and Proclamation

"Death and life are in the power of the tongue, and those who love it will eat its fruit." **(Proverbs 18:21)**

Declaration: An affirmation; an open expression of facts or opinions; verbal utterance of one's sentiments.

Proclamation: An official notice given to the public; to announce, publish or promulgate; to declare with honor.

Our words that we speak are very powerful. We must speak life to the land we occupy. We have been called to stand in the gap for the land. This is done through repentance and intercession. We must marry and rededicate the land to the Lord and then God will protect it (Isaiah 62: 4-7). I have done this in the county I reside in as well as the property my home sits on. The righteous must stand in the gap for the land. The blood of Christ has made many righteous in America. They must stand and declare and proclaim that the land is God's. We are able to bless the Lord with our words and break curses off the land.

*"I looked for a man among them who would build up the wall and **stand before me in the gap on behalf of the land so I would not have to destroy it**, but I found none. So I will pour out my wrath on them and consume them with my fiery anger, bringing down on their own heads all they have done, declares the Sovereign Lord."* **(Ezekiel 22: 30-31)**

Is it possible we are living in the days of Jeremiah and Ezekiel? They prophesied that God could bring disaster on a nation if it continued to choose to walk in disobedience and its own ways.

*"The instant I speak concerning a nation and concerning a kingdom, to pluck up, to pull down, and to destroy it, if that nation against whom I have spoken turns from its evil, **I will relent of the disaster that I thought to bring upon it**. And the instant I speak concerning a nation and concerning a kingdom, to build and to plant it, if it does evil in My sight so that it does not obey My voice, then **I will relent concerning the good with which I said I would benefit it**. Now therefore, speak to the men of Judah and to the inhabitants of Jerusalem, saying, Thus says the LORD: Behold, I am fashioning a disaster and devising a plan against you. **Return now every one from his evil way**, and make your ways and your doings good. And they said, "…We will walk according to our own plans, and we will every one obey the dictates of his evil heart."* **(Jeremiah 18: 7-12)**

We *(radical remnant)* must seek the Lord and His will first (prayer closet) and hear what is on God's heart regarding the land. **When the Spirit of God bears witness with the human spirit then He gives power for us to proclaim.** Intercession then becomes proclamation. **The church has authority by proclaiming the will of God.** We must be in agreement with heaven. God is looking for people who will be in agreement with His heart! Surrendering our will to God's plans for the land or any given situation will bring results.

"Seek the Lord and His strength; Seek His face evermore!" **(1 Chronicles 16:11)**

Point to Ponder: "Every revival starts because of God and every revival ends because of man" - Bill Johnson

• 9 •

BUILDING THE HOUSE OF FAITH!

*"According to the grace of God which was given to me, **as a wise master builder** I have **laid the foundation**, and another builds on it. But let each one **take heed how he builds** on it. For **no other foundation can anyone lay than that which is laid, which is Jesus Christ**. Now if anyone builds on this foundation with gold, silver, precious stones, wood, hay, straw, **each one's work will become clear**; for the day will declare it, because it will be revealed by fire; and the fire will test each one's work, of what sort it is. If **anyone's work which he has built** on it endures, he will receive a reward. If anyone's work is burned, he will suffer loss; but he himself will be saved, yet so as through fire. Do you not know that **you are the temple of God** and that the Spirit of God dwells in you?"* **(1 Corinthians 3: 10-16)**

FOUR PILLARS IN THE HOUSE OF FAITH

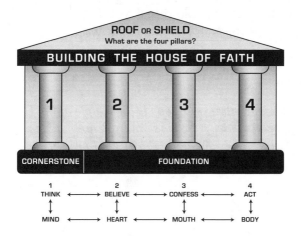

> **Point to Ponder:** Whatever you **think** on with your mind will result
> in a **belief** system within your heart. Whatever you believe in your
> heart you will **confess** or speak with your mouth. Your **actions** (body)
> will soon follow as you live out what is in your heart. Your nature and
> character will be formed and your destiny determined.

Give Honor to where it is Due!

Soon after I became a Christian, I was fortunate to be connected
with one of the best Bible teachers and fathers of the faith I had ever
encountered. His name was Bob Reid. His teaching on the **"house
of faith"** greatly impacted my walk with the Lord. Bob instructed
me through example to live by faith, and he planted seeds that would
eventually lead me to fulfill my vision and destiny. He receives full
credit for this inspiring revelation in God's Word on the house of
faith. Through the years I was able to **add insights** given to me by
other men and women in the body of Christ.

You Are a Spiritual House

After you become born again, God is anxious to build an everlasting
spiritual house within you. **You are "God's house" and "His
temple."** God will allow you to work together with Him so your
spiritual house will be eternal and you can face any challenges that
come your way. Within this spiritual house, God will cast vision and
destiny so you will have the opportunity to live your life of fulfilling
the purpose of God's kingdom that you have been called to. God
chooses to do this through His Spirit and Word.

*"Unless the **Lord builds the house**, its builders labor in vain"*
(Psalm 127:1)

*"Or do you not know **that your body is the temple of the Holy Spirit who
is in you**, whom you have from God, and you are not your own? For you
were bought at a price; therefore glorify God in your body and in your
spirit, which are God's."* **(1 Corinthians 6:19-20)**

It Takes Faith to Build a Spiritual House

God works with man one by one applying faith principles (2 Corinthians 5:7), and He is not a respecter of persons (Acts 10:34, Galatians 3:26). So whether you are a man or woman, young or old, member of any race, we all have an opportunity **to activate the measure of faith** (Romans 12:3) God planted in each and every one of us. Faith is a force that is waiting to materialize. Living by faith is supposed to be a normal way of life. Faith is the surrender to God's will and plans for any situation. We must be like little children (Matthew 18:3) as we approach God, yet it says we are soldiers (2 Timothy 2: 3-4). We can fight as soldiers but realize we are sons and daughters of God (Ephesians 1: 4-5).

> **Point to Ponder:** "Out of a very intimate acquaintance with D. L. Moody, I wish to testify that he was a far greater prayer than he was preacher. Time and time again, he was confronted by obstacles that seemed insurmountable, but he always knew the way to overcome all difficulties. He knew the way to bring to pass anything that needed to be brought to pass. He knew and believed in the deepest depths of his soul that nothing was too hard for the Lord, and that **prayer could do anything that God could do.**" - R. A. Torrey

This measure of faith gives us the ability and capacity to accomplish great things. Since we are created in God's image (Genesis 1:26), we are a faith being. **Jesus said,** *"Have faith in God"* (Mark 11: 22-23). **Yet man bases his faith on his five senses.** It is a mentality that says, *"I have to see it to believe it!"* There is another dimension that exists that the eye cannot see. The whole world is held together by God's Word and power (Hebrews 1: 2-3). The unseen world consists of subatomic particles, atoms, and molecules. Everything consists of particles and energy. **We are particle beings.** The Spirit of God created all matter and is held together by that same Spirit.

*"In the beginning **God created the heavens and the earth**. The earth was without form, and void; and darkness was on the face of the deep. And the Spirit of God was hovering over the face of the waters."* **(Genesis 1: 1-2)**

Since God's Spirit controls all matter, it is the greater authority over the lesser authority. **The world around us must yield to that greater authority.** God's people can take the world's kingdoms by force. It is through faith where we must learn to rule and reign with the Spirit of God. The material world that is around us must become subject to God's Word. We must shift our awareness and align ourselves with the promises of God and **see how things ought to be.** Do not allow your environment and circumstances to limit you! Learning to walk in the image and presence of God releases massive potential where you will see the Goliaths of life falling down before you. Nothing can stop you from overcoming any challenge.

> **Point to Ponder:** "If we would pray aright, the first thing we should do is to see to it that we really get an audience with God that we really get into His very presence. Before a word of petition is offered, we should have the definite consciousness that we are talking to God, and should believe that He is listening and is going to grant the thing that we ask of Him." - R.A. Torrey

When we become susceptible to doubt, it destroys our faith. **"Faith" is in the present tense** as we serve a God who is on the move. Will you move with God in what He has planned for your life? Your faith can be looked at as a **"title deed"**, or can be referred to as purchasing power because of the work of the Cross. Faith takes hold of things you hope for (vision and destiny) and makes them a reality.

God has given man authority on the earth to move the impossible, change circumstances, and create. We are allowed to work with God, as God anoints diligence, obedience, and preparation. As we walk on life's path, God wants to co-create with us. He gives each of us permission to design things around desires that the Holy Spirit has placed in us. These desires are a force that attracts God's favor and what He wants to do for you.

> **Point to Ponder:** Why don't we doubt our doubts and believe God instead?

STEP 1 - The Cornerstone and Foundation

We start with the cornerstone and the foundation:

CORNERSTONE [1 Peter 2:7]	FOUNDATION [1 Corinthians 3: 9-16] *"If the foundations are destroyed what can the righteous do?"* [Psalm 11:3]

*"Therefore, to you who believe, He is precious; but to those who are disobedient, **The stone which the builders rejected Has become the chief cornerstone.**"* **(1 Peter 2:7)**

*"For we are God's fellow workers; you are God's field, **you are God's building.** According to the grace of God which was given to me, as a wise master builder I have **laid the foundation**, and another builds on it. But let each one take heed how he builds on it. **For no other foundation can anyone lay than that which is laid, which is Jesus Christ.**"* **(1 Corinthians 3: 9-11)**

The foundation of every house must be solid in order to build on it. Whether it's a physical or spiritual house, the foundation must be adequately laid. The Bible clearly states that a house built on sand will end up destroyed when storms come.

*"Through **wisdom** a house is built, and by **understanding** it is established;"* **(Proverbs 24:3)**

*"Therefore whoever hears these sayings of Mine, and does them, I will liken him to a wise man **who built his house on the rock**: and the rain descended, the floods came, and the winds blew and beat on that house; and **it did not fall, for it was founded on the rock**. But everyone who hears these sayings of Mine, and does not do them, will be like **a foolish man who built his house on the sand**: and the rain descended, the floods came, and the winds blew and beat on that house; **and it fell**. And great was its fall."* **(Matthew 7: 24-27)**

We each are a spiritual house (1 Corinthians 3: 9-11). The **individuals in "the church" comprise a larger corporate house.** The scripture declares we are living stones that make up a larger spiritual house (1 Peter 2:5). This spiritual house has a cornerstone and foundation.

Our belief systems or foundation that has been laid will eventually determine a nation's rise and fall. If America has a strong moral foundation (Jesus Christ) built on the principles of the Word of God, the people living in that nation will prosper and be free. If these moral foundations are destroyed, then good people will suffer.

*"If the **foundations are destroyed**, what can the righteous do?"*
(Psalm 11:3)

Point to Ponder: Many churches are not temples made of living stones; they are piles of living stones that have not been built into anything. Many Christians get stolen away as they have not been cemented into place. We need to build people spiritually – line by line, precept by precept and then it will be difficult to pry them out of their place!

Every properly built house needs a foundation. How firm is the foundation of your spiritual house? For Christians, Jesus Christ is the only foundation that can be built upon that will last and withstand any storm. It is the only foundation that can bring salvation, deliverance from sin, healing, fulfilled vision and destiny, etc. The finished work of Jesus Christ on the cross is the perfect foundation.

The Cornerstone of the House of Faith

What is a cornerstone? It is a key stone in the foundation, providing the essential and necessary strength upon which we must build. Jesus Christ, who is the Word of God, is that cornerstone (Acts 4: 10-12). He contains everything God wants you to think and know, learn and understand, and to speak and act on. So the foundation and cornerstone have been laid – Jesus Christ. The Word of God is the cornerstone and it stands alone (John 4: 23-24, 8:32, 17:17).

*"Now, therefore, you are no longer strangers and foreigners, but fellow citizens with the saints and members of the household of God, having been built on the foundation of the apostles and prophets, **Jesus Christ Himself being the chief cornerstone**, in whom the **whole building**, being fitted together, **grows into a holy temple in the Lord**, in whom you also are being built together **for a dwelling place of God** in the Spirit."*
(Ephesians 2: 19-22)

*"Coming to Him as to a living stone, rejected indeed by men, but chosen by God and precious, you also, as living stones, **are being built up a spiritual house**, a holy priesthood, to offer up spiritual sacrifices acceptable to God through Jesus Christ. Therefore it is also contained in the Him will by no means be put to shame. Therefore, to you who believe, He is precious; but to those who are disobedient, **The stone which the builders rejected has become the chief cornerstone** and a stone of stumbling and a rock of offense."* **(1 Peter 2: 4-8)**

Are you ready to **continue building** your spiritual house of faith? Let's erect the pillars!

STEP 2 - The Thinking Pillar

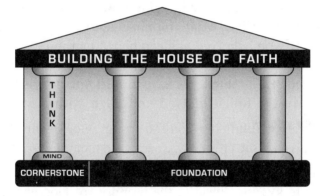

Thought: A thought is a collection of ideas on which the mind dwells. It is where the mind is directed to a subject or objects and stretches to it to form conceptions.

Imagination: The power or faculty of the mind by which it conceives and forms ideas of things communicated to it by our five senses. It is to form ideas and representations in the mind by our will working on the materials of memory. It selects parts of different conceptions or objects from memory to form a whole more pleasing than has ever been presented in the ordinary course of nature. This same mind can also take the whole idea formed and make it terrible or awful as well.

This pillar involves your thinking, thoughts, and imagination. God never asked you to "kiss your brain goodbye" when you received Jesus Christ as your personal Savior. God said to let us reason together (Isaiah 1:18) and that His people perish for lack of knowledge (Hosea 4:6). God wants us to grow in the grace and knowledge of the Lord, Jesus Christ (2 Peter 3:18). Every bit of God's Word is directed toward your intelligence so you can read, hear, listen, and converse with Him. Faith comes by hearing, and hearing the Word of God (Romans 10:17).

Point to Ponder: "Our prayers lay the track down which God's power can come. Like a mighty locomotive, His power is irresistible, but it cannot reach us without rails." - Watchman Nee

---

Your thoughts lead to your imagination, and this is the key to changing your reality! What you imagine today you will receive tomorrow – if you believe. Faith can play a part in receiving what you hope for. The environment you are in will be drawn to the reality that is formed in your mind. We have to **shift our imagination into confidence in the Spirit of God and align with His promises**. Doubt is our enemy!

The book of Hebrews 11 is known as the "hall of faith." Individuals like Abraham, Isaac, Jacob, Joseph, Moses, Rahab, Gideon, and Samson were looking ahead to the promises of God and believed them. They saw the promises far off in their mind, were persuaded, assured, and embraced them! Their minds were filled with their imagination of the promises of God, and that caused them to take a stand in what were sometimes very adverse circumstances.

*"**By faith** Abraham obeyed when he was called to go out to the place which he would receive as an inheritance. And he went out, not knowing where he was going. **By faith** he dwelt in the land of promise as in a foreign country, dwelling in tents with Isaac and Jacob, the heirs with him of the same promise; for **he waited** for the city which has foundations, whose builder and maker is God. **By faith** Sarah herself also received strength to conceive seed, and she bore a child when she was past the age, because **she judged Him faithful** who had promised. Therefore from one man, and him as good as dead, were born as many as the stars of the sky in multitude — innumerable as the sand which is by the seashore. **These***

all died in faith, not having received the promises, but having seen them afar off were assured of them, embraced them and confessed that they were strangers and pilgrims on the earth." **(Hebrews 11: 8-13)**

We are God's sons and daughters. Meditate on this until it becomes part of you! We **must build our thought process to where we can imagine what it would be like to be touched by the presence of God.** We have a better covenant today, with even better precious promises.

Point to Ponder: Your imagination has no concept of time and does not exist in time. It says, "what if it could be true?" This is the place where faith can become a substance if the imagination can engage God's promises. The kingdom of God, which is out of time and available to us at all times, can change reality which is held in time. So bring into your imaginations the kingdom of God and His precious promises! If you have faith, (believe, desire, and do not doubt in your heart) your reality will change.

As your mind is renewed and transformed, God has something to work with, and He will begin to release vision and destiny, or your assignment in life. God is after your eye and ear gates because He wants access to your mind and heart. God will bring perfect peace to your mind as you develop an intimate relationship with Him (Isaiah 26:3-4). He has given you a free will to think about good or evil things. You will become whatever you allow your mind to dwell on.

"For as he thinks in his heart, so is he." **(Proverbs 23:7)**

Point to Ponder: "Each time, before you intercede, be quiet first, and worship God in His glory. Think of what He can do, and how He delights to hear the prayers of His redeemed people. Think of your place and privilege in Christ, and expect great things!"
- Andrew Murray

Your thoughts **feed your imagination**, which paints a picture (good or bad) in your mind of the manifestation and reality you are looking for. An inner hope begins to develop that is a confident idea of what you expect to happen. In Genesis 6:5, we see the imaginations of men's hearts were continually evil, so God destroyed the world. **These evil imaginations became a reality** and God had to visit and intervene in their affairs. The capacity is within us to think about good things and imagine life from God's perspective. If we are to **cast down evil imaginations, why not lift up good ones instead?**

*"For the weapons of our warfare are not carnal, but mighty through God to the pulling down of strong holds; **Casting down imaginations**, and every high thing that exalts itself against the knowledge of God, and **bringing into captivity every thought** to the obedience of Christ."* **(2 Corinthians 10: 4-5)**

Body - Soul – Spirit

We each are a body, soul and spirit - a threefold being. How does this affect our house of faith? The body is our flesh and the spirit is our conscience, the intuitive knowledge of God and the place of communion with Him. The soul consists of our mind, will and emotions. God communes with our spirit but we are caretakers of our soul. Our soul operates in the earth realm. There is a battle for it (1 Peter 2:11). Our greatest possession is our soul. We try to invest in everything else but God wants our souls to proper (3 John 2). The soul is what gets in the way of walking in the spirit.

*"Then Jesus said to His disciples, "If anyone desires to come after Me, let him deny himself, and take up his cross, and follow Me. For whoever desires to save his life will lose it, but whoever loses his life for My sake will find it. For what profit is it to a man **if he gains the whole world, and loses his own soul? Or what will a man give in exchange for his soul?*** **(Matthew 16: 24-26)**

God considers souls precious! He who wins souls is wise (Proverbs 11:30). We are to pray for them. The thinking pillar in the house of faith must be understood in relation to the soul of man. We are able to impact the souls of men which consist of the **mind, will, and emotions** of those around us.

The Mind and the Will of Man

We are to renew our minds in Christ as it affects our will or choices we make. Are we walking in the promises of God or not? Man has a sovereign free will and can resist God. Your free will can resist men around you. God doesn't interfere with the will of man because true love will not result if he is made to obey. We are not robots as God is not a respecter of persons. If God favors the will of one man He is responsible to do it for all. If a challenge or hurtful situation confronts us we need to be in a position to know God so well (relationship) so we can hear to get out of the way. God wants to impart wisdom to us so we can avoid the minefields of life.

The Placebo Affect and the Will

Have you ever heard of the placebo affect? A substance such as sugar pills would be given in place of the actual medication in a test group. The results proved to be better in the placebo group. What was this saying? The mind is a very powerful force to overcome those things that <u>have no will</u>. The mind was telling the patient they were better because of the medication even though there was none. If we can grasp that **the mind and will of man can overcome those things that do not have a will** our prayers will change our surroundings. What would be a hindrance that circumvents us?

My own will is what prevents me from moving in the promises of God. **The enemy is after our souls** (thinking pillar). He wants our mind so we will operate out of negative emotions that can result in bad choices. So we must choose to resist the devil - a choice of the will. Our own will must forcefully be put into place in order to be effective in praying for others.

*"Therefore submit to God. **Resist the devil and he will flee from you.** Draw near to God and He will draw near to you. Cleanse your hands, you sinners; and purify your hearts, you double-minded."* **(James 4: 8-9)**

Something that can say "no" can say – **"yes"**. We have the authority to change one's life as priests of God. Prayer brings the favor of God upon the souls of men. He will influence their lives because we have intervened in their behalf. It will take importunity, persistence and discipline in many cases.

Point to Ponder: Have you ever seen an out of control child that affects the whole family dynamic? The will of that child is so strong that it causes much strife in the family. The will must be brought into subjection by loving discipline and then peace will result.

Dealing with the soul is very important so we can allow the kingdom of God to run our spirit life. There is a freedom knowing that something that doesn't have a will cannot resist God. Jesus cursed the fig tree (Matthew 21: 19-21). He said speak to the mountain and it shall be removed (Mark 11:23). **Anything that does not have a will cannot resist me.** I have authority in Christ. If our will is surrendered to God He will act in our behalf. Remember, **disease has no will!** Those dealing with issues in life have authority over them (Hebrews 4:16). **Pornography has no will.** We can overcome any challenge if our house of faith is constructed properly. We are not to worry about what we are to eat or drink (Matthew 25: 26-34). God will supply our needs as we speak the word over those things that do not have a will.

Learning from the Centurion

This passage (Matthew 8: 5-13) in the Bible has more to do than with **faith and authority**. There is a third aspect. Disease has no will. Jesus told the centurion who had a will to go. The centurion obeyed and he went. Yes, the centurion moved by faith in the authority he was given, but those things **(disease) that had no will** had to move out of the way. His servant was healed! We must get beyond the point in thinking what is holding people in bondage is greater than the ability we have to free them. The prayer closet of the *radical remnant* is where this revelation can be released.

Getting Around Mans Will

So how can we get around man's will? We must realize that Jesus is the same in the past, present and future. We have the authority to deal with the past and future that affects the present. We can be time travelers in the Lord.

"Jesus Christ is the same yesterday, today, and forever." **(Hebrews 13:8)**

Issues in the past have no will. We can pray not only for ourselves but those in our sphere of influence to break down the bondages holding them. These individuals who had a will in the past no longer have that will because it is in the past. **You have authority over it.** They have no will in the future so you can speak life giving words for them. You can set up detours and roadblocks so wrong choices can be hindered. Have you ever heard of a prophetic word? One of the purposes of prophecy is to bring into being what God has given for one's life. We can call those things to be as they ought to be. Dealing with the past and future opens doors to shape a man in the present **as he still has a will.** God's favor and hand will be upon them.

Discoveries in Quantum Physics

Quantum physics is the study of things so small that we cannot see them, yet everything we observe is made of these subatomic particles. Recent discoveries in quantum physics are proving what the Bible already states. The area we occupy, or the atmosphere and field we exist in, is impacted by our thoughts. We exist in this five sense realm, yet fail to see the other dimensions we are part of (unseen world). Your thoughts can make you well or sick, happy or depressed, and change your mood or attitude. Your thoughts have the capacity to send out messages and affect the environment in which you live.

Research has proven emotional states are even transferable. One person can light up a room with joy or create an atmosphere of doom and gloom. **This can be done without saying anything.** Words are energy and energy affects matter. When you articulate how you feel and what you are thinking, **it can be life or death to those around you.** Have you ever thought of someone and all of a sudden they called on the phone? There is an unseen world we need to better understand as there is a definite spiritual connection.

Point to Ponder: Thoughts and beliefs you carry produce energy around you. It affects the people you are around. When you feel love or anger in a person the atmosphere changes.

Research has shown how a visible force field of atoms seen by the naked eye can be changed by our thoughts. When you spin an atom one way it will affect and cause others to spin in that same direction. Atoms also have strings which are vibrating constantly. Even a solid rock is vibrating. If a group of **faith filled** individuals are praising God in one accord in one place, **will heaven take notice?** Of course!

Even the foods we consume have energy fields that are picked up by modern day instrumentation. Vegetables give off life while other foods have little life in them (fast food burgers for example have no life). Everything is connected by force fields and we are able to impact them by faith. The field of quantum physics has also discovered that **sound has weight and force**. Jesus said to speak to the mountain and it shall be removed (Mark 11: 21-23). Faith-filled spoken words do have an effect. God spoke the world into existence as it was framed by His Word. **When your thoughts, internal convictions, and belief systems converge into a godly agreement, there is a force released that can bring the kingdom of God to earth.** Everything is connected in the universe, and this awesome God we serve knows when a sparrow falls to the ground, as well as every hair that is on your head.

Point to Ponder: When you have a purpose in life that is backed by burning desire, it creates a frequency that eliminates obstacles and draws the necessary resources to make it a reality.

Thoughts and Unbelief

So how important is believing and having faith when you pray? Our thoughts determine the state of our heart and internal convictions. Jesus could perform few miracles in His home town **because of unbelief** in the people. We see here how important unbelief and faith are in regards to answered prayer.

"But Jesus said to them, 'A prophet is not without honor except in his own country, among his own relatives, and in his own house.' **Now He could do no mighty work there,** *except that He laid His hands on a few sick people and healed them.* **And He marveled because of their unbelief.***"* (Mark 6:4-6)

Scientific studies are indicating that **your thoughts and what you say** can cure cancer (epigenetics) as well as other afflictions. It is also being discovered that various sounds can change the human genome and impact our attitudes and emotions. Harp music has been found to lower blood pressure and reduce anxiety. Isn't it interesting that David played the harp to calm down King Saul when he faced an "anxiety attack." (1 Samuel 16:23).

As we take a closer look at Luke 8:49-56, we see an account where a young girl died. Jesus said to believe and all will be well. He went to the girl, who was lying on a bed with three of His disciples and her parents. Jesus said she was not dead but sleeping, and the parents ridiculed Him. Then Jesus sent all of them out of the room and put His hand upon her and told her to arise, and she did. The parents were astonished. Why did Jesus send them out of the room? Did they lack faith? Would they be a hindrance to what Christ was about to do? **I have to wonder how the atmosphere is affected by unbelief.** Is this the reason we do not see the manifestation of healing and then wonder why?

> **Point to Ponder:** Have you ever attended a game when a team was playing with great tenacity and confidence, where they knew they could not lose and emotions were running high? Their excitement gripped everyone present. What about a group of individuals who believe in God's Word in a **supercharged atmosphere of faith**? When we come to this place, the supernatural – accompanying signs and wonders will manifest.

Offenses Hinder Answered Prayer

I hope you are seeing how creation is so interconnected. Christians are members of one body and we affect each other. **Offenses, divisions,**

strife, unbelief, and doubt can affect those all around us. I have to believe that church splits and contention among members in the body do more harm to the advancement of the kingdom of God than we realize.

"Casting lots causes contentions to cease, and keeps the mighty apart. A **brother offended is harder to win than a strong city,** *and contentions are like the bars of a castle."* **(Proverbs 18: 18-19)**

Can you see why so many marriages break up over unresolved conflict? The atmosphere is charged with anger, strife, jealousy, where wounded hearts are venting on one another. An individual who has been hurt speaks from emotional upset which temporarily may seem right (and feel good) but actually worsens the situation. As they attempt to resolve the issues at hand they are still charged with negative emotions. Quick impulsive and destructive decisions are made that widen the breech. God has a better way!

Point to Ponder: What about racism in the church? The devil's plan is to cause division at all levels in our culture. The African American, White, Hispanic, and Asian Christian churches must come together. We are all made new creatures in Christ (2 Corinthians 5:17). If we are made new creatures and the old has passed away **we must lose our culture.** The color of our skin is of no consequence as we are all in Christ. Our identity is in Jesus. There is neither Jew nor Greek, bond or free, nor male or female (Galatians 3:28) but we are one in Christ. We are really **masquerading as humans** in this flesh body. Racism in the church affects how prayers are answered in the body of Christ.

What about **church splits or contention** within a church body? Many times control issues on both sides of the offense are the root of the problem. In communities across this nation church splits and strife have occurred within church bodies. I unfortunately have been part and even caused a church split. So I can speak from experience. I have repented of every one and have done everything possible to make things right. It is through this experience I realize how super charged an atmosphere can become because of tensions. This is a sure way to hinder answered prayer and short circuit the vision and destiny of a church, ministry, or individual.

"That there should be no schism in the body, but that the members should have the same care for one another. And if one member suffers, all the members suffer with it; or if one member is honored, all the members rejoice with it." (**1 Corinthians 12:25-26**)

"But now indeed there are many members, yet one body." (**1 Corinthians 12:20**)

It never ceases to amaze me how we can know the scriptures yet not act upon them. Love and forgiveness are central parts of the Gospel. When in the heat of emotions we can become blind and believe we are acting in God's will yet not apply His Word. We can say we forgive and have let things go but instead accuse or condemn. I have done this myself! **We serve a God of reconciliation and restoration.**

"And be kind to one another, tenderhearted, forgiving one another, even as God in Christ forgave you." (**Ephesians 4:32**)

Man has the tendency to self justify his actions. Where there is strife and contention there is judgment and accusation. So how can you bring these people who profess Christ back together? It will take humility, childlikeness, and a passion to be like Christ. It is sitting down and blessing people who may have cursed you. Can praying a blessing result in correction? Yes! Let's stop accusing and saying this person has a devil or hasn't really repented. It is the enemy of our souls who desires offense as he knows prayers will not be answered. We must strive for unity in the body of Christ.

Point to Ponder: Your physiological and emotional makeup sends out frequencies (speaking scientifically) that can impact your surroundings. Fear and anger are just as contagious as some disease causing virus or bacteria. Studies have shown that one moment of fear or anger will sap us of more energy than hours of hard labor. Offenses drain the human spirit as well and can spread quickly from one person to the next.

What about unbelief, lack of faith, and offenses? Do you see a correlation here? The challenges we face are those **inner voices** and that internal dialogue that oppose what God's Word says. The unseen world of Quantum physics is affected by our thoughts, spoken words, emotions, beliefs and how we act. There must be an internal conviction that God's Word and promises are true. **Mixed messages between your mind (thoughts) and what you believe in your heart produce mixed results.** This is called double mindedness (James 1: 6-8).

We do not want to limit God. We each have to deal with these challenges that life presents. Look at them as opportunities to be Christ like and may we defeat those thorns that are in the harvest field we have been called to labor in. Wherever unbelief, lack of faith and offenses have surfaced expect that God will intervene in your behalf. Make that appeal and He will answer and your thinking will be realigned.

> **Point to Ponder:** "Beware in your prayers, above everything else, of limiting God, not only by unbelief, but by fancying that you know what He can do. Expect unexpected things 'above all that we ask or think'." - Andrew Murray

STEP 3 - The Believing Pillar

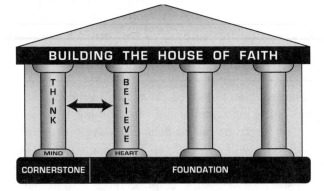

Our belief system can be a hindrance or a launching pad into our destiny. This pillar consists of our heart, inner being, motives, intentions, ambitions, and emotions. It is the **file cabinet** where we store everything – good or bad.

"Do you not yet understand that whatever enters the mouth goes into the stomach and is eliminated? But those things **which proceed out of the mouth come from the heart,** *and they defile a man.* **For out of the heart proceed evil thoughts,** *murders, adulteries, fornications, thefts, false witness, blasphemies."* (**Matthew 15: 17-19**)

After you meditate and think about God's Word, you must have faith and believe in it. As a son or daughter in Christ, you have inherited precious promises because of what Jesus Christ accomplished on the cross. All of our thinking must be converted into believing what God's Word declares and then settled in our heart. Believing in what God's Word proclaims will bring transformation and will further build **the house of faith** (Matthew 21:21-22)

"Jesus said to him, **If you can believe, all things are possible to him who believes."** (**Mark 9:23**)

"Most assuredly, I say to you, **he who believes in Me, the works that I do he will do also; and greater works than these he will do, because I go to My Father.** *And whatever you ask in My name, that I will do, that the Father may be glorified in the Son.If you ask anything in My name, I will do it."* (**John 14: 12-14**)

Point to Ponder: One of the reasons people encounter difficulty in believing prayer can move a mountain in our life is that it sometimes takes a long time for things to manifest. If you plant a seed in a garden do you dig it up each day to see if it has grown?

What are the life passions that drive you? What are your desires? What is it you want and don't have? Your passions and desires can be flesh or spirit! Identify them and you will begin to discover what foundation your belief system is built on. Desire is what connects you to what God wants you to do. We understand that **sin can be conceived through desire** (James 1: 12-16). **Why then not God's plans?**

Desire: Emotion or excitement of the mind directed at the attainment or possession of an object from which sensual, intellectual, or spiritual gratification or pleasure is expected. It is a passion excited by the love of an object.

*"My **heart grew hot within me**, and as **I meditated, the fire burned**; then I spoke with my tongue."* **(Psalm 39:3)**

*"And Jesus answering said unto them, have faith in God. For verily I say unto you, That whosoever **shall say unto this mountain**, be thou removed, and be thou cast into the sea; and **shall not doubt** in his heart, **but shall believe** that those things which he said shall come to pass; **he shall have whatsoever he said**. Therefore I say unto you, **What things soever ye desire**, when ye pray, **believe that ye receive them**, and ye shall have them."* **(Mark 11: 22-24)**

Point to Ponder: The eye and ear gates to our heart must be guarded. Thinking can be shifted in small subtle increments, and you can come under the influence of another belief system or ideology that opposes the nature and character of God.

In Luke 8: 40-48, we see a woman who was healed of a blood disorder, and Jesus commented it was **her faith** that made her whole. She came to Christ and touched His garment and knew that He had healing power. She totally believed and had no doubt. What about the Roman Centurion who believed in the authority that Christ had for his servant to be healed (Matthew 8: 5-13)? Jesus saw his great faith. We must be convinced that what we are doing is walking by faith. Allow the Word of God to define who we are. Do you walk by faith or by sight? Let's continue on to build the House of Faith.

Point to Ponder: "The Bible is not an end in itself, but a means to bring men to an intimate and satisfying knowledge of God, that they may enter into Him, that they may delight in His Presence, may taste and know the inner sweetness of the very God Himself in the core and center of their hearts." - A.W. Tozer

STEP 4 - The Confessing Pillar

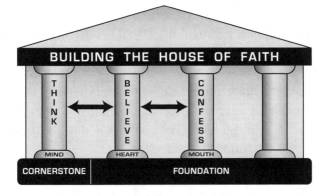

There is **life and death in the power of your tongue** (Proverbs 18:21). The words that you speak can bring health, encouragement, joy, and life to a person. **Studies have shown that any negative word spoken needs two to five positive words to negate the effects upon a person.** What you speak and declare, coupled with faith, can also determine the success of your walk with the Lord and the effectiveness of your ministry for God. It involves much more than quoting a Bible verse.

There has to be an agreement with God's Word and His truth that is in your heart. Your **inner voices** can speak at the same time and contradict the Bible promise given to you. Many of us have **an ongoing war with strongholds of unbelief.** You may pray for someone to be healed, but voices inside are saying, *"God doesn't heal,"* or *"It must not be God's will for this person,"* or *"God wouldn't use me."*

Point to Ponder: Principles of faith and confession that Jesus taught may seem to be nonsense to some. This worldly point of view does not operate in the laws of the kingdom of God. We are not of this world (John 17:16). God gave us the keys to the kingdom so open what God has given to you.

We must instead **speak** our **faith filled words** that are **in agreement** with God's Word, where there is no doubt and unbelief. **Those inner**

voices must be quenched so the force of favor is released in you.
As you speak, see things as they ought to be and not how they appear
to be! These internal voices, or scripting, come from the old unre-
generate man and past personal history. It is what we can refer to as
the "old you," as opposed to the new creation you are called to be in
Christ. These voices have authority and they can break an agreement
with God's Word. They come against the very desires and hopes in
your prayers. These internal voices are beliefs and thoughts lodged
in your heart as strongholds. They **cause a double mindedness**,
where we receive nothing from God.

*"But let him **ask in faith, with no doubting**, for he who doubts is like a
wave of the sea driven and tossed by the wind. For let not that man suppose
that he will receive anything from the Lord; **he is a double-minded man**,
unstable in all his ways."* (**James 1: 6-8**)

Can you remain optimistic through conflict and be content in all
challenges that test your faith? Out of the abundance of your heart
you will **speak life or death**. Can those internal voices be stilled?
You can have expectations or desires for the future, but if those in-
ternalized voices or intentions are not speaking the same, they will
be an anchor and keep you from going anywhere.

> **Point to Ponder:** Your external and internal confession exposes
> whether you have faith or doubt! What is your confession?

Confession is both inward and outward! **That constant inner
dialogue that takes place in your mind must be reigned in.** This
dialogue that comes out of our heart must not oppose what we
should be doing. What you say externally or internally can be either
a hindrance to a higher calling you have, or an encouragement to
seek new heights. The lies must be dismantled, past personal history
crucified on the cross, and the strongman bound in Jesus' name
(Mathew 13: 28-29). The cleansing stream of God's grace and Word
can make new any past challenge, difficulty, or struggle.

> **Point to Ponder:** Studies done at a university in Minnesota have

shown we think at a pace of 1500 words per minute of internal dialogue. Eighty percent is unconscious. We may not be aware what we are speaking in our thoughts. Whatever dominates your mind's focus will dominate you. So what you say to yourself is very powerful. Check on how you are feeling, or your present state of emotion. Jesus said when things are bad, look to Him. We have the capacity to change our thinking and internal confession patterns!

*"For by your **words you will be justified, and by your words you will be condemned.***" (**Matthew 12:37**)

*"Let us hold fast **the confession of our hope without wavering**, for He who promised is faithful"* (**Hebrews 10:23**)

God spoke the world into existence. So again, begin to speak and see things as they will be and do not dwell on what is not. **Bring the kingdom of God into your imagination and it will become a reality.** Try to see the seed of vision that God has planted in you coming alive and bearing fruit. What farmer plants a field with seed and doesn't have the expectancy of a great harvest!

This is not a magical New Age formula but principles and rules of the Spirit that the church needs to grasp. The pillars of the house are going up. It all began with the foundation and the cornerstone. **The thinking, believing, and confessing pillars were erected.** The last pillar is the acting pillar. Then the roof can be put on, which is your shield of faith.

STEP 5 - The Acting Pillar

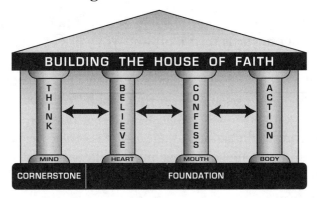

As God opens doors, you must go through them with His direction and guidance. It is most certainly a journey where challenges will abound. As God speaks to you, you must listen and **act on the directives** He gives you. We are running a race, walking by faith, and must be doers of the Word. In order for the water to part or in order to obtain answers to prayer, steps are taken in faith. The key to this process is being certain that you *truly heard from God*. This is where intimacy and a relationship with God come in. After you make the decision to act, be sure all alternatives and other options are cut off.

Point to Ponder: "I have seen many men work without praying, though I have never seen any good come out of it; but I have never seen a man pray without working." - James Hudson Taylor

---

Many times people will act on self-originated plans that are not God's wishes at all. Ask the Lord for a confirmation and be patient. David made it a habit to inquire of the Lord. Good works must follow our faith and this faith works by love (Galatians 5:6)

*"What does it profit, my brethren, **if someone says he has faith but does not have works?** Can faith save him? If a brother or sister is naked and destitute of daily food, and one of you says to them, 'Depart in peace, be warmed and filled,' but you do not give them the things which are needed for the body, what does it profit? Thus also faith by itself, if it does not have works, is dead. But someone will say, 'You have faith, and I have works.' **Show me your faith without your works, and I will show you my faith by my works.'"* **(James 2: 14-18)**

Faith always requires corresponding action. **Many times it can mean moving towards the unknown.** Will you step into the water before it parts? Will you go into a land that is filled with enemies and take it for the purposes of God's kingdom? Do you believe that God will go before you and act on your behalf? Will you act in such a way that you know God has answered your prayers? Your inner desires will result in action if there is a passionate desperation. It begins with the thoughts in your mind, beliefs in your heart, and what you speak with your mouth. This congruency will manifest in answers to prayer and fulfilled destiny.

*But **be doers of the word, and not hearers only**, deceiving yourselves. For **if anyone is a hearer of the word and not a doer**, he is like a man observing his natural face in a mirror; for he observes himself, goes away, and immediately forgets what kind of man he was. But he who looks into the perfect law of liberty and continues in it, and is not a forgetful hearer **but a doer of the work**, this one will be blessed in what he does"* **(James 1: 22-25)**

As you move forward in God's purposes, He will protect you and put a roof (shield) on your House of Faith, in which you will be able to stand against the fiery darts of the enemy. If God is for you, who can be against you?

STEP 6 - The Roof and Shield of Faith

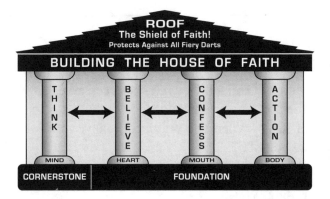

Every house needs a roof! A roof provides protection from all the outside elements if properly constructed. It makes you feel secure when a storm approaches. The roof on our "house of faith" is what we call the **shield of faith**.

*"**Therefore take up the whole armor of God, that you may be able to withstand in the evil day**, and having done all, to stand. Stand therefore, having girded your waist with truth, having put on the breastplate of righteousness, and having shod your feet with the preparation of the gospel of peace; above all, **taking the shield of faith with which you will be able to quench all the fiery darts of the wicked one**."* **(Ephesians 6:13-16)**

*"The **Lord is my strength and my shield**; my heart trusted in Him, and I am helped;"* (**Psalm 28:7**)

All the names of God and the inheritance we have in the cross because of the shed blood of Jesus Christ make up the roof in our **"house of faith"**. God is our peace, shepherd, provider, righteousness, healer, banner, and the One who is always there for us. You are saved by faith, so bury this in your hearts.

Point to Ponder: "It is in the field of prayer that life's critical battles are lost or won. We must conquer all our circumstances there. We must first of all bring them there. We must survey them there. We must master them there. In prayer we bring our spiritual enemies into the Presence of God and we fight them there. Have you tried that? Or have you been satisfied to meet and fight your foes in the open spaces of the world?" - J. H. Jowett

---

THE NAMES OF GOD AND YOUR INHERITANCE IS YOUR COVERING

You are an adopted child of God who has been given an inheritance! These are the precious promises of God and what is represented in the name of Jesus. When you pray and believe in His name, these promises are yours!

Yahweh – The I AM, or the self-existent One (Exodus 3:14, 15:2; Psalm 46:1, 68:4; Malachi 3:6).

Elohim – The all-powerful One (Genesis 1:1-3; Deuteronomy 10:17; Psalm 68; Mark 13:19).

Immanuel – God with us (Isaiah 7:14, 8:8-10; Matthew 1:23).

Jehovah-Rapha – The Lord who heals (Exodus 15:25-27; Psalm 103:3,147:3; 1 Peter 2:24).

Jehovah-Nissi – The Lord is my banner (Exodus 17:15-16; Isaiah 11:10-12; Ephesians 6:10-18).

Jehovah-Jireh – The Lord is my provider (Genesis 22:13-14; Psalm 23; Mark 10:45).

Jehovah-Shalom – The Lord is my peace, my wholeness and totality in life (Numbers 6:22-27; Judge 6:22-24; Hebrews 13:20).

Jehovah-Rohi – The Lord is my shepherd (Psalm 23:1-3; Isaiah 53:6; John 10:14-18).

Jehovah-Shammah – The Lord is there (Ezekiel 48:35; Psalm 46; Matthew 28:20).

Jehovah-Tsidkenu – The Lord our righteousness (Jeremiah 23: 5-6, 33:16; 2 Corinthians 5:21).

Jehovah-Mekkaddishkem – The Lord who sanctifies (Exodus 31: 12-13; Hebrews 13:12).

Jehovah-Saboath – Lord of hosts and armies (1 Samuel 3:17, 45; Psalm 46:7; Romans 9:29).

Point to Ponder: "What greater rebellion, impiety, or insult to God can there be, than not to believe his promises?" -- Martin Luther

• 10 •

TOUCHING GOD'S HEART IN PRAISE AND WORSHIP

---

*"I will **praise You with my whole heart**; Before the gods **I will sing praises** to You. **I will worship** toward Your holy temple, And **praise Your name**. For Your loving kindness and Your truth; For You have magnified Your word above all Your name."* **(Psalm 138: 1-2)**

*"Give unto the Lord the glory due to His name; **worship the Lord** in the beauty of holiness."* **(Psalm 29:2)**

Prayer/Praise/Declaration and Worship

Understanding the importance of prayer, praise, declaration and worship is a key to any Christian's walk – and the prayer closet movement of the *radical remnant*. They convey intimate communication with God. It is not just prayer, praise, declaration, and worship but – **"desperate prayer, passionate praise, faith filled declaration, and heart rendering worship"** – that makes available to us all the promises of God because of what Jesus Christ accomplished on the cross. Prayer, combined with praise, declaration and worship, will develop an intimacy with God where His presence will be felt. This type of relationship, cultivated in this atmosphere, will enable us to fulfill our destiny and make history because God is acting in our behalf.

"Praise Him for His mighty acts; **Praise** *Him according to His excellent greatness!* **Praise** *Him with the sound of the trumpet;* **Praise** *Him with the lute and harp!* **Praise** *Him with the timbrel and dance;* **Praise** *Him with stringed instruments and flutes!* **Praise** *Him with loud cymbals;* **Praise Him** *with clashing cymbals! Let everything that has breath* **praise** *the LORD.* **Praise** *the LORD."* **(Psalm 150:1)**

Point to Ponder: "Yes, worship of the loving God is man's whole reason for existence." - A.W. Tozer

---

Praise the Lord

We have sure used this phrase "praise the Lord" many times. It is wise to have an understanding of this word as true worship of God will resonate from our praises. There is no Hebrew word found for praise in the book of Psalms. There are seven Hebrew words that convey what <u>praise</u> is though. As you look at these various words we must ask if this is what is truly taking place in our corporate church settings. Is this taking place in our prayer closets? The good news is that a deeper understanding is being revealed and the church - the *radical remnant* - is responding with true praise. Biblical praise will draw the presence of God.

Hebrew Words for Praise

YADAH: To worship with an extended hand; the giving of oneself in worship and adoration; to lift your hands unto the Lord which carries the meaning of absolute surrender as a child to his parent when he asks to be picked up.

TEHILLAH: It is to sing a **spontaneous new song** or singing from a melody in your heart by adding words to it. This refers to a special kind of singing. It is singing unprepared, unrehearsed songs. This brings tremendous unity to the body of Christ and it is singing straight to God where it connects the heart of man with the heart of God. It is the **praise that God inhabits** (Psalm 22:3). God manifests Himself in the minds of those who exuberantly sing.

BARAK: It means to kneel or to bow and give reverence to God as an act of adoration. It implies to continually give a conscious place to God as we bless the Lord and extol His virtue.

HALAL: It means to shine; to make a show, to boast and thus to be (clamorously) foolish; it is to rave and be causative, to celebrate; act madly; become unglued.

TOWDAH: It is a display of worship by the extension of the hand in adoration or agreeing with what has been done or will be. It is the giving of thanks or praise as a sacrifice before reception or manifestation. We are to thank God for something that I don't have in the natural. It is an agreement with His Word and faith in His Word - especially if one is very sick in body. The carnal mind would fight and ridicule this particular action, but there is great faith in TOWDAH as praise as this symbolizes agreement.

ZAMAR: It is where singing with instruments and making music accompanied by the voice; it also means to touch the strings, and refers to praise that involves instrumental worship. It's usually translated "sing praises".

SHABACH: To address in a loud tone, a loud adoration, a shout! Proclaim with a loud voice, unashamedly, the GLORY, TRIUMPH, POWER, MERCY, and LOVE OF GOD. This word implies that testimony is praise. The phrase **"shout unto the Lord"** can be understood as the action of SHABACH. It is not just being loud. You should have the attitude of putting your whole being into it, an attitude of being totally uninhibited.

The Power of Unified Sound

Across America I see increased stirrings and rumblings where the church is bringing forth a sound that is resonating with one voice going up before God. I was stirred in the late nineties by a man of prayer - Lou Engle. Since that time I see the corporate prayer movement growing. It is a process and I am an optimist that the prayers that have gone up have bought time for our nation.

"Indeed it came to pass, **when the trumpeters and singers were as one,** **to make one sound to be heard in praising and thanking the LORD,** *and when they lifted up their voice with the trumpets and cymbals and instruments of music, and* **praised** *the LORD, saying: For He is good, For His mercy endures forever, that the house, the house of the LORD, was filled with a cloud, so that the priests could not continue ministering because of the cloud; for* **the glory of the LORD filled the house of God.***"*
(2 Chronicles 5:13-14)

We have now entered a day of greater understanding where music and song, combined with the prayers of the saints, moves the hand of God. **True praise, declaration, and worship will bring the presence of God into our midst.** We need his visitation and revelation! We have the opportunity here on earth to join with heaven as multitudes praise him day and night before His throne (Revelation 4:8). A symphony of one sound on earth will unite with the sounds of heaven before God's throne.

There is a **power in sound** that affects the atmosphere around us. It has weight and force. Heavenly revelation is presently being given to us regarding the dynamics of quantum physics in relation to sound and light. When music, declarative song, and prayer are combined the matter which makes up all of creation is affected.

Point to Ponder: Our worship, praise and prayers can be better defined as touching the throne of God. Never let them lose its appeal because God allows us to come before Him on a regular basis. If it was possible that the stars would only come out one night each year, we would make a point to see them because of the beauty of a clear night sky. How much more excited should we be in coming before the one God who created the stars?

Three Sounds Resonating Across the Earth at this Time:

1. The prayers from the house of Islam in the five-a-day prayers going across the world, chants and meditations of false philosophies and religions of the world, and witchcraft and paganism.

2. The sound of the secular media, entertainment, movies,

television, the Internet, arts, and communication systems. It professes humanism and an anti-Christ philosophy.

3. A "House of Prayer," is rising in our nation and the world, crying out to God in Jesus' name. There is a unity in our diversity that is uncompromising, where singers, musicians, intercessors, watchman, and all who pray are gathering together.

The church is now rising to where its prayers, voice, and declarations will be heard. The voice of the Lord will shake the wilderness (Psalm 29: 7-9). We have been given the opportunity through prayer, praise, and worship to be a voice upon the earth to **impact the world we live in**. The closets of prayer where the *radical remnant* individually seek the Lord must now rise to the next level. Light will dispel the darkness that is on the earth. We are the Lord's voice on the earth and what we say can bring life or death.

*"The **voice of the Lord divides the flames of fire**. The **voice of the Lord shakes the wilderness**; The Lord shakes the Wilderness of Kadesh. The voice of the Lord makes the deer give birth, and strips the forests bare; and in His temple everyone says, Glory."* **(Psalm 29: 7-9)**

We are partners and have been given the opportunity to co-labor with God. The world is presently shaking off its false foundations, and we have an opportunity to take dominion.

*"And from the days of John the Baptist until now the kingdom of heaven suffers violence, and the **violent take it by force**."* **(Matthew 11:12)**

The New Song

*"Rejoice in the Lord, O you righteous! For **praise** from the upright is beautiful. **Praise the Lord with the harp**; **Make melody to Him** with an instrument of ten strings. **Sing to Him a new song**; Play skillfully with a shout of joy.* **(Psalm 33: 1-3)**

God is raising up a *radical remnant* of musicians and singers. They are **singing and musical priests**. They are being called to bring a **"new song"** and sound that is out of God's heart. These songs will bring the Jonah's of today out of the belly of the whale. These new songs will break old cycles and old ideas. The musicians will use their instruments to play and sing the name of God into the moment. We are in a time where you may play one song for an extended period of time until the meaning and power of those words are released into the atmosphere. The creative power of God can manifest in this song as there is focus and agreement. **You continue to sing the song until God can speak through it.** This is "tehillah praise". It is where prayer and songs of the spirit inhabits our whole being.

What am I trying to say? The way we perceive music in the present day church should be looked at and changed as we study the Biblical definitions of the word praise. Regions can be changed by the corporate unity of musicians, singers and the praying *radical remnant*. There are frequencies in a unified voice and sound that can change people, transform regions, and move the nations of the earth. Can a frequency be created where disease could not exist? There is no disease in heaven. There is no fear or anger in heaven. If the **"new song"** comes from heaven the earth has to shake and move and come into alignment with it. No matter how dark it gets a more powerful sound in the **"new song"** is available. Light will burst forth from these musicians and singers.

Point to Ponder: "God wants to change our song. When we come into agreement with what the enemy says about us that becomes our song. If we come into agreement with what God says that will be our song." - Ray Hughes

---

NOTE: Pastors and leaders have difficulty at times relating to musicians and singers in the church. At times there is a element of control where the goal is to have an organized good church service. The musicians and singers may feel they are operating in a box where there is little freedom. In saying this there has to be a **respect of authority** and understanding of pastoral responsibility. There has to be communication and both sides must seek the Lord. Do not allow offenses to manifest as disunity and contention is not conducive for the Holy Spirit to move.

The Tabernacle of David is being Rebuilt

So what is this Tabernacle of David? Is it to be rebuilt (Amos 9:11)? Where and how is it to be rebuilt? The tabernacle of David is a place where God's throne is established, spiritual offerings are being made, and where we present ourselves as a living sacrifice. Jesus Christ dwells (John 1:14 – tabernacled with us) in our hearts, and when we come together as one to pray, praise, and worship Him, the presence of God is in our midst. His presence will draw in the lost as the hearts of men melt before Him.

*"After this I will return **And will rebuild the tabernacle of David**, which has fallen down; **I will rebuild its ruins**, And I will set it up; So that **the rest of mankind may seek the LORD**, Even all the Gentiles who are called by My name, Says the LORD who does all these things."* (**Acts 15: 16-17**)

King David had appointed 4,000 singers and musicians for service in the Tabernacle (1 Chronicles 23:5). During his reign, they prayed and sang praises 24 hours a day, seven days a week. The Ark of the Covenant was present. For 33 years there were no wars. We are living in a day where the prayer movement in our nation is escalating. Houses of prayer are manifesting where 24/7 prayer, praise, and worship are continually ascending before God's throne. If our nation is to be saved, it lies in the hope of desperate prayer, faith filled declaration, passionate praise, and adoring worship of our God and King. **The personal prayer closet where individuals seek the Lord will ignite corporate prayer gatherings to new levels.** These prayer warriors and lovers of God will come with hot burning hearts that have experienced intimacy with the Lord. The *radical remnant* is a direct part of the rebuilding of the Tabernacle of David. There is a company of **singing and musical priests** stepping into a calling for this day.

*"Now when He had taken the scroll, the four living creatures and the twenty-four elders fell down before the Lamb, **each having a harp, and golden bowls full of incense, which are the prayers of the saints**. And **they sang a new song**, saying: "You are worthy to take the scroll, And to open its seals; For You were slain, And have redeemed us to God by Your blood Out of every tribe and tongue and people and nation, And have*

made us kings and priests to our God; *And we shall reign on the earth."* **(Revelation 5: 8-10)**

Young people from our nation are presently connecting to a very potent prayer movement. Generations are coming together. The gap between denominations is being bridged. God is calling forth a *radical remnant* of young worshippers of God that are aligning with the older generation. The Lamb who became the Lion is on the move!

"Then another angel, having a golden censer, came and stood at the altar. ***He was given much incense, that he should offer it with the prayers of all the saints*** *upon the golden altar which was before the throne.* ***And the smoke of the incense, with the prayers of the saints,*** *ascended before God from the angel's hand. Then the angel took the censer, filled it with fire from the altar, and threw it to the earth. And there were noises, thunderings, lightnings, and an earthquake."* **(Revelation 8: 3-5)**

Point to Ponder: How many people have attended church services and sang the various worship songs and repeated every word correctly and do not remember what they were singing about? Wouldn't it be better to focus your thoughts as you sing, and picture in your mind the majestic awesomeness of God, His love, and His mercy so it would burn hot within your heart?

• 11 •

SOME FUNDAMENTAL ASPECTS OF PRAYER

Let us now consider various aspects that involve prayer. God in His Word has very clearly stated and given us guidelines regarding effective prayer. Jesus certainly fulfilled the conditions, and He was our immediate example. We must lay the proper foundational aspects of prayer so our own spiritual house is in order.

*"If the **foundations are destroyed,** what can the righteous do?"* **(Psalm 11:3)**

Our righteousness is in Jesus Christ, and His shed blood (atonement) is what gives us access to the Father. We must gain a deeper revelation of what Jesus accomplished. Most in the church have not grasped nor have gained a sense of awe as well as reverence for what the cross provided for us. To say we serve a big God is one thing but to understand how big He is can be hard to grasp. The gift of salvation for eternity must never be taken for granted and understated. The "prayer closet" time will become more meaningful when we realize that we are scarcely saved and it was only through His love for us.

*"For the time has come for judgment to begin at the house of God; and if it begins with us first, what will be the end of those who do not obey the gospel of God? Now "**If the righteous one is scarcely saved**, where will the ungodly and the sinner appear?"* **(1 Peter 4: 17-18)**

Fear of the Lord

We see the phrase **"fear of the Lord"** very frequently in the Bible. Stop and carefully consider what the scriptures are saying when you come across this phrase. How does it relate to our prayers? No prayer closet can be fruitful without a clear and concise understanding of what is being said in that one simple phrase - fear the Lord!

*"My son, if **you receive my words**, and **treasure my commands** within you, so that you **incline your ear to wisdom**, and **apply your heart to understanding**; yes, if you **cry out for discernment**, and **lift up your voice for understanding**, if you **seek her as silver**, and **search for her as for hidden treasures**; then you **will understand the fear of the Lord**, and find the knowledge of God."* **(Proverbs 2: 1-5)**

Early in my Christian walk I noticed Proverbs 2: 1-5 and saw a number of criteria to understand the fear of the Lord. I realized my prayer closet and devotional times were a key to obtain understanding regarding answered prayer. The secret place is the place of searching, seeking, inclining our ear, applying our hearts, lifting our voice, and crying out.

*"The angel of the Lord encamps all around those **who fear Him**, and delivers them. Oh, taste and see that the Lord is good; blessed is the man who trusts in Him! Oh, **fear the Lord**, you His saints! There is no want to those **who fear Him**. The young lions lack and suffer hunger; but those who seek the Lord shall not lack any good thing. Come, you children, listen to me; I will teach you the **fear of the Lord**."* **(Psalm 34: 7-11)**

*"Behold, the eye of the Lord is on those **who fear Him**, on those who hope in His mercy, to deliver their soul from death, and to keep them alive in famine."* **(Psalm 33: 18-19)**

*"He will fulfill the desire of those **who fear Him**; He also will hear their cry and save them."* **(Psalm 145:19)**

*"The **fear of the Lord** leads to life: then one rests content, untouched by trouble."* **(Proverbs 19:23)**

What does this word fear mean in the context given in the above scriptures? Are we supposed to fear God the one whom the Bible says clearly loves us? The word **fear means to be in a <u>reverential awe</u>. It is moral respect and regard given to the creator of the universe.** It is a realization that your life is in His hands as well as recognition of the sacrifice made for you. The prayer closet is enhanced when entering it with the fear of the Lord. It is not the same fear that the ungodly will have when coming before our God as they shake and tremble.

Point to Ponder: "Shut the world out, withdraw from all worldly thoughts and occupations, and shut yourself in alone with God, to pray to Him in secret. Let this be your chief object in prayer, to realize the presence of your heavenly Father." - Andrew Murray

---

*"For it is written: as I live, says the Lord, **every knee shall bow to Me, and every tongue shall confess** to God."* (**Romans 14:11**)

Can you imagine what it will be like for those who are unsaved as they stand before God and have denied the Son Jesus Christ? The realization of eternity in Hell will come before them and a different kind of fear will set in that **will shake the core of the inner man.** It is literally indescribable. It is for this reason the prayer closet is important. We must make appeals for those who are lost in this dying world.

*"And as **it is appointed for men to die once, but after this the judgment,** so Christ was offered once to bear the sins of many. To those who eagerly wait for Him He will appear a second time, apart from sin, for salvation."* (**Hebrews 9: 27-28**)

But those who are saved in Jesus Christ will be overwhelmed with thankfulness and joy. There will be a revelation of how big and powerful God really is. This reverential awe is what brings man to say Holy, Holy, Holy, Lord God almighty!

Answered Prayer is Conditional

We serve a God that desires to answer prayer, but we must realize there are conditions we must meet to obtain His favor. **A surrendered life, and living to be set apart for God in humility, is certainly**

the place to begin. When we seek his face and pray while walking in repentance and forsaking our sins, God's ears are open to our cries. Many Christians backslide. They are unable to stand against the temptations of the world, or the bondages of their old nature. They strive to do their best to fight against sin, and to serve God, but they have no strength. **What has led to this condition?** They have never really grasped the secret of the prayer closet. The Lord Jesus every day from heaven will continue His work in me. But on one condition - **the soul and spirit must give Him time each day to impart His love and grace.** Time alone with the Lord Jesus each day is the indispensable condition of growth and power.

*"I thank my God upon every remembrance of you, always in every prayer of mine making request for you all with joy, for your fellowship in the gospel from the first day until now, being confident of this very thing, that **He who has begun a good work in you will complete it until the day of Jesus Christ;"*** **(Philippians 1: 4-6)**

*"Then the Lord appeared to Solomon by night, and said to him: **I have heard your prayer**, and have chosen this place for Myself as a house of sacrifice. When I shut up heaven and there is no rain, or command the locusts to devour the land, or send pestilence among My people, if My people who are called by My name **will humble themselves, and pray and seek My face, and turn from their wicked ways, then I will hear from heaven, and will forgive their sin and heal their land.** Now My eyes will be open and My ears **attentive to prayer made** in this place."* **(2 Chronicles 7: 11-15)**

Point to Ponder: "If the Christian does not allow prayer to drive sin out of his life, sin will drive prayer out of his life. Like light and darkness, the two cannot dwell together." - M.E. Andross

---

As righteousness exalts a nation (Proverbs 14:34) living righteously will exalt our spiritual house. Have we established a new set of righteousness which does not resemble the one God requires? I have labored over this question many times. **Our righteousness is established in Jesus Christ**, but there is a responsibility to obey and carry out God's will on the earth. It is a life of walking by faith and repentance (turning from sin).

*"For He made Him who knew no sin to be sin for us, that **we might become the righteousness of God in Him.**"* (**2 Corinthians 5:21**)

*"The **Lord rewarded me according to my righteousness;** according to the cleanness of my hands He has recompensed me. For **I have kept the ways of the Lord, and have not wickedly departed from my God.** For all His judgments were before me, and I did not put away His statutes from me. I was also blameless before Him, and **I kept myself from my iniquity.** Therefore the Lord has recompensed me **according to my righteousness,** according to the cleanness of my hands in His sight."* (**Psalms 18: 20-24**)

*"Do you not know that to whom you present yourselves slaves to obey, you are that one's slaves whom you obey, whether of sin leading to death, or of **obedience leading to righteousness?** But God be thanked that though you were slaves of sin, yet you obeyed from the heart that form of doctrine to which you were delivered. And having been set free from sin, you **became slaves of righteousness.** I speak in human terms because of the weakness of your flesh. For just as you presented your members as slaves of uncleanness, and of lawlessness leading to more lawlessness, so now **present your members as slaves of righteousness for holiness.**"* (**Romans 6: 16-19**)

The righteousness we are to live in **is one of godly moral character.** We are to love our fellow man. We are to carry out God's will here on earth as it is in heaven. We are not speaking of good works to earn a right to be heard but a works that naturally comes from being in the presence of the Lord.

*"Then Peter opened his mouth and said: In truth I perceive that God shows no partiality. But in every nation **whoever fears Him and works righteousness** is accepted by Him."* (**Acts 10: 34-35**)

Point to Ponder: "Prayer - secret, fervent, believing prayer - lies at the root of all personal godliness." - William Carey

---

Other Hindrances to Answered Prayer

There are other hindrances to answered prayer such as selfishness (Ephesians 4: 22-24), sin (Psalm 66:18), walking in disobedience (1 John 3:21), pride (Proverbs 16:18), and not honoring our wives (1 Peter 3:7). These can be overcome by the grace of God (Hebrews

4:16). Our prayers can also be hindered by spiritual warfare (Daniel 10), as there is a hierarchy of demons that war over people and nations (Ephesians 6: 10-18). As Daniel prayed, angels came to his assistance and battled for him as they are all ministering spirits (Hebrews 1: 13-14; Matthew 4:11).

*"The **angel of the Lord encamps** all around those who fear Him, and delivers them."* **(Psalm 34:7)**

> **Point to Ponder:** "Depend upon it, if you are bent on prayer, the devil will not leave you alone. He will molest you, tantalize you, block you, and will surely find some hindrances, big or little or both. And we sometimes fail because we are ignorant of his devices... I do not think he minds our praying about things if we leave it at that. What he minds, and opposes steadily, is the prayer that prays on until it is prayed through, assured of the answer." - Mary Warburton Booth

What about Faith and Patience?

The aspects of faith and patience are key principles, It is impossible to please God without faith (Hebrews 11:6). **We must also be patient (Hebrews 6:12) and realize that answers to prayer can be instantaneous (miraculous) or progressive over time.** God is sovereign. The church has a general ignorance of how answers to prayer can be progressive. So people have a tendency to doubt, get discouraged, lose hope and finally give up. There much be a persevering patience coupled with faith.

Defiled Land

The land we occupy needs also to be healed, as the scripture reference in 2 Chronicles 7:14 indicates. The blessings of God and answered prayer will not manifest upon a land that has been defiled. What curses are on the land because of Free Masonry, broken covenants, worship of false gods, pagan rituals, unresolved offenses, abortion and the taking of innocent life? We repeatedly read about Kings in the Old Testament who walked in disobedience and did not tear down the altars of false gods. Some even built altars to false idols that surrounding cultures worshipped.

*"In the seventeenth year of Pekah the son of Remaliah, Ahaz the son of Jotham, king of Judah, began to reign. Ahaz was twenty years old when he became king, and he reigned sixteen years in Jerusalem; and **he did not do what was right in the sight of the Lord** his God, as his father David had done. But he walked in the way of the kings of Israel; indeed he **made his son pass through the fire**, according to the abominations of the nations whom the Lord had cast out from before the children of Israel. And **he sacrificed and burned incense on the high places**, on the hills, and under every green tree."* (**2 Kings 16: 1-4**)

We live in a vapor or spot of time in history. God is merciful but also just. In my short tenure on this earth I can do much to plead for the land so we as a nation can be spared from judgments. This is one of the purposes of the *radical remnant*. Can I pray for those in authority over me so God can move on those in our behalf? Yes! May we not be distracted by the cares of life and be taken away from the potential we have through prayer.

Is it the people who defile the land because of disobedience and walking unrighteously? Yes! Lack of prayer has opened the doors for wickedness to gain a foothold. So we must point our fingers at ourselves first. As we stand in the gap for the land (Ezekiel 22:30) we must closely examine the condition of our own hearts first. We must surrender all that is displeasing to our God and by faith receive God's forgiveness. Then **deal with the land** you reside in - by faith.

*"Asa did what was good and right in the eyes of the Lord his God, **for he removed the altars of the foreign gods and the high places**, and **broke down the sacred pillars** and **cut down the wooden images**. He commanded Judah **to seek the Lord God of their fathers**, and **to observe the law and the commandments**. He also **removed the high places and the incense altars** from all the cities of Judah, and the kingdom was quiet under him. And he built fortified cities in Judah, for the land had rest; he had no war in those years, because the Lord had given him rest."* (**2 Chronicles 14: 2-6**)

It will take faith to turn back the tide of evil that is upon our land. It will take faith to break those curses. It will take faith to free the land from false gods. We need God's wisdom to identify them and move in faith that comes by hearing and hearing the Word of God (Romans

10:17). **It is in the prayer closet** where God can instill His mind and will in you. It is the place where confidence will be imparted to walk by faith and agree with others of like mind to intercede for the land.

Point to Ponder: "It is not enough to begin to pray, nor to pray aright; nor is it enough to continue for a time to pray; but we must patiently, believingly, continue in prayer until we obtain an answer; - George Müller

---

Are we Praying Correctly? - Think about it!

The first mention of prayer in the Bible is Genesis 4:26, where men began to **"call"** upon the Lord. In the original Hebrew language, every letter represented a picture symbol. It was like reading a comic strip! Three Hebrew letters make up the word *call* in Genesis 4:26 and they represent the front of a head, back of a head, and an ox putting his head into a yoke. A Hebrew individual reading this would see **a turning of the head to face the one who can take the burden**. What does that remind you of? Jesus sits at the right hand of the Father interceding (Romans 8:31-39) for us. He is the one who takes and bears our burdens.

Point to Ponder: Prayer invokes the authority to close the gates of Hell and open the windows of Heaven. Rise up and take your place as a King and Priest (Revelation 1:5-6)

Westerners do not pray like the Hebrew mindset did. **We do a lot of talking but never fully comprehend what we have prayed for.** To build a passion and desire in our heart for what we are asking, we **must think about what we pray for and let our imagination build a picture of what we are hoping for.** This is where your faith can become a substance! In other words, can you see in your mind what you are praying for? Can you take the kingdom of God and His precious promises and bring them into your imagination and have faith so your reality can be changed? We can do this!

*"Now faith **is the substance of things hoped for**, the evidence of things not seen."* **(Hebrews 11:1)**

Example Prayer to Consider: "God, protect my son, who is in law enforcement."

Meditate on a prayer instead of moving on to the next one until you become passionate for the need you have brought before God's throne. So I would picture my son sitting in his police car, with an angel at each side as well as in the front and back. I would picture his face in my mind, seeing God speaking into his ear, giving him wisdom in the decisions he has to make. Actually "see" what you are praying for and meditate on it until your desire increases. **Emotions result from what you think on and what is gripping your heart.** This does require some discipline on our part but how bad do we want results regarding the things we make requests for.

In Genesis 6:5, God saw that the imaginations and thoughts in men's hearts were always evil. This resulted in a generation of people who walked in total disobedience to God, and the world was destroyed (Noah's flood) as a result. Evil is born from what we think about (Matthew 12: 33-37, 15: 16-20). **Desires and passions become a substance, or materialize and become actions.** Our repeated actions will build habits and develop our nature then character and will determine our destiny (James 1: 12-16). Evil hearts will result in and produce evil fruit. We can see this process at work regarding evil, **but why not see it regarding good?**

Example Prayer to Consider: "Please heal my mother of cancer."

Focus your mind on Christ the healer and his promises. Reflect on the stories in the Bible where people laid hands on the sick and they recovered. Literally see these accounts in your mind and then picture your mother being ministered to by Christ. See the cancer being removed. Faith is a substance of things hoped for and evidence of things not seen. Picture your mom walking upright, whole, well and rejoicing. This is **bringing the kingdom of God into your imagination to change the reality of the situation** you are facing. In other words believe this scripture in Hebrews 11:1.

NOTE: I heard a testimony about a woman who had inoperable cancer on her leg. It would take her life. No human remedy could bring any positive result. What she did was buy a CD player with headphones and placed the headphones on her leg. She played worship and praise music continually with the sound penetrating that leg. Over a period of time the cancer was gone! This may sound strange to many but when in dire straits I would do the same.

THE LORD'S PRAYER (Matthew 6: 9-13): How should we pray this perfect prayer?

As we look at the Lord's Prayer, instead of speaking it out quickly, break it down into parts and build into your imagination what is being prayed. Rabbis call it an index prayer. **It is intended to open up our minds to vast realms of understanding of who God is** and what He represents to us.

The Lord's Prayer	Picture in Your Mind
Our Father	His presence
Who art in heaven	His position
Hallowed be thy name	His preeminence
Thy kingdom come	His power
Thy will be done on earth	His purpose
As it is in heaven	His pattern
Give us this day our daily bread	His provision
Forgive us our trespasses and	His pardon
Lead us not into temptation	His protection
For Thine is the kingdom and glory	His praise and worship

When opening the prayer with "Our Father," take a breath and pause, and see Him as *your* Father. He is represented as compassionate and merciful as opposed to being a dictator. When we say "who art in heaven," we must picture in our mind that there is one who sits on the throne of the universe ruling and reigning. The various names of God must come to the forefront of our thoughts when we say "hallowed be thy name." He is our healer, peace, banner, provider, righteousness, and shepherd as well as much more.

Point to Ponder: Prayer should not be regarded "as a duty which must be performed, but rather as a privilege to be enjoyed, a rare delight that is always revealing some new beauty." - E.M. Bounds

---

If you can grasp what is being taught above, it will revolution-ize your prayer life in the prayer closet. Your circumstances will change as **God's kingdom invades your reality**. Faith will become a substance and evidence of things not seen.

*"Have **faith** in God. For assuredly, I say to you, whoever says to this mountain, 'Be removed and be cast into the sea,' and **does not doubt in his heart, but believes** that those things he says will be done, he will have whatever he says. Therefore I say to you, whatever things you ask when you pray, **believe that you receive them**, and you will have them."* **(Mark 11: 22-24)**

Assurance that God Answers Prayer

Faith and doubt do not mix. **Doubt your doubts and believe God!** We must have faith and believe that we will receive what we ask for. God wills it and He is bound by His Word to answer your prayers. It is also a demonstration of His deity and a sign of God's supernatural power.

When prayers are not answered, we must point the finger at ourselves and not God. Quiet and still those inner voices that speak to your mind against what God has promised. We have been given dominion and authority over the land we occupy and have the inheritance of the cross as **adopted sons and daughters**. In the atonement (Isaiah 53) we have been given privileges.

Point to Ponder: God answers our prayers because He loves us. He is merciful, compassionate, kind, and desires to take care of His children (Psalm 145:8).

God hears your prayers if you can tune into heaven's realm. We must rid ourselves of the static of distraction, unbelief and apathy! In any room, there are numerous radio frequencies in the air. You have the availability to pick up a news show, sports, and various types of music. This is what is called the quantum or natural realm. Everything consists of particles, atoms, waves, light, and sound as previously discussed. **There is a frequency from heaven called the God channel – in the prayer closet.** So tune in! It is a place where you are heard and heaven is opened.

"At this also my heart trembles, And leaps from its place. **Hear attentively the thunder of His voice, and the rumbling that comes from His mouth. He sends it forth under the whole heaven,** *His lightning to the ends of the earth. After it a voice roars;* **He thunders with His majestic voice and** *He does not restrain them when His voice is heard. God thunders marvelously with His voice; He does great things which we cannot comprehend."* **(Job 37: 1-5)**

God's voice has gone to the ends of the earth. He speaks to us in many ways if we are willing to listen. We must adjust from a self awareness to God awareness. Tune in to the "dialogue frequency" where God is speaking to His people. This is the same frequency **where prayers are heard**. It is called the third heaven.

Point to Ponder: "Faith in a prayer-hearing God will make a prayer-loving Christian." - Andrew Murray

---

Importance of Agreement

The Apostle Paul knew of a man caught up or taken to the "third heaven" (2 Corinthians 12:2), who had an experience that could not be expressed in words. This is the realm where God dwells and where Satan was cast out (Luke 10:18-19; Revelation 12:9). We live in the first heaven, or earthly realm. Satan dwells in the second heaven and has access to earth. **When we pray, we must ask ourselves what we are in agreement with** – the frequency of the third heaven (Word of God) or the second heaven (lies of Satan).

Agreement: Concord, unity, harmony, or conformity to an opinion or sentiment.

*"Can two walk together, **unless they are agreed?**"* (**Amos 3:3**)

If we desire answers to prayers, we must be in agreement with the author and finisher of our faith. **The second heaven is the "static" that attempts to block God's voice and answers to prayer.** When Daniel prayed for revelation (Daniel 10: 10-14), Michael the Archangel was sent (from the third heaven). Michael encountered the Satanic Prince of Persia (second heaven) for 21 days, who attempted to stop the answer of Daniel's prayer from getting back to Daniel (first heaven or earthly realm). This resistance is what we face today in different forms. **Agreement with God's Word by faith is critical to receive answers to prayers.** God's frequency has a small, still voice that we are able to tune into. The distractions (static) of the second heaven must be eliminated!

We must learn to feel the truth of the third heaven and then we can build our lives in the Spirit. Build an awareness of Christ and the inheritance He has given us and release it on others, as well as yourself. Be assured that God is looking out for your well-being. Prayer is grabbing hold of the throne of God and tapping into all of its heavenly resources.

Point to Ponder: "Prayer is not overcoming God's reluctance, but laying hold of His willingness" - Martin Luther

---

Praying with Importunity

An area that inhibits answered prayer in the Western world is lack of persistence and patience. **We want things right now and immediately in the modern culture.** Is there a price to pay? Do we need to earn the right to be heard? Is there more in the spiritual realm that is taking place than meets the eye? Do we give up too easily? Importunity is a condition of prayer!

*"Then He spoke a parable to them, **that men always ought to pray and**

*not lose heart, saying: There was in a certain city a judge who did not fear God nor regard man. Now there was a widow in that city; and she came to him, saying, Get justice for me from my adversary. And he would not for a while; but afterward he said within himself, Though I do not fear God nor regard man, yet **because this widow troubles me** I will avenge her, lest **by her continual coming she weary me**. Then the Lord said, Hear what the unjust judge said. **And shall God not avenge His own elect who cry out day and night to Him,** though He bears long with them? I tell you that He will avenge them .speedily. Nevertheless, **when the Son of Man comes, will He really find faith on the earth?**"* **(Luke 18 1-8)**

*"Rejoice always, **pray without ceasing**, in everything give thanks; for this is the will of God in Christ Jesus for you."* **(1 Thessalonians 5: 16-18)**

Importunity is an aspect of prayer that we need to seriously consider. We see it mentioned in both Old and New Testaments. It is not "vain repetitions"– but something else – **urgent repetitions**. It does not exhibit a lack of faith. So what is importunity?

Importunity: It is a pressing solicitation or an urgent request. It's an appeal for a claim or favor, which is urged with troublesome frequency or pertinacity. It is a frequent demand.

Point to Ponder: Have you ever gone fishing? When a fish gets hooked it begins to fight for its survival to escape being caught. After the hook is set the line must be kept tight with no slack as any slackness gives the fish the opportunity to shake out or spit the hook out. When we pray for people it is like fishing. When the Holy Spirit grabs hold of any individual and shakes them in their circumstances they begin to fight and may experience much turmoil (as a hooked fish). We must not let up in our prayers (slack in the line) as we are trusting that God is working on them. Never give up in your prayers for people whom God has put on your heart. It will take importunity!

I have witnessed the birth of my four children and observed my wife in labor. The pushing began as the baby traveled down the birth canal. With every contraction there was an urgency to bring forth that new life. As the babies head crowned, the final pushes were initiated by my wife, and the joyous birth resulted. It was not easy, but it was labor intensive. So it goes with labor in the "prayer closet" for the lost and the desires of one's heart to manifest. **It is a pressing in and never giving up where by faith you know that you know what you asked for will come.**

Point to Ponder: "We can do nothing without prayer. All things can be done by importunate prayer. That is the teaching of Jesus Christ". - E. M. Bounds

---

"And He said to them, which of you shall have a friend, and go to him at midnight and say to him, 'Friend, lend me three loaves; for a friend of mine has come to me on his journey, and I have nothing to set before him'; and he will answer from within and say, 'Do not trouble me; the door is now shut, and my children are with me in bed; I cannot rise and give to you'? I say to you, though he will not rise and give to him because he is his friend, **yet because of his persistence he will rise and give him as many as he needs. Keep Asking, Seeking, Knocking so I say to you, ask, and it will be given to you; seek, and you will find; knock, and it will be opened to you.** *For everyone who asks receives, and he who seeks finds, and to him who knocks it will be opened."* **(Luke 1: 5-10)**

Point to Ponder: When looking at a stone cutter hammering away at a rock a hundred times without so much as a crack showing in it. Yet at the 101st blow it splits in two. I know it was not the one blow that did it, but all that had gone before.

The best knockers will prevail with God. It will be those with prevailing faith who will petition the throne of God unceasingly. It's where a heart cries out because of the pain it feels or the desperation to see a loved one saved.

"O Lord, God of my salvation, **I have cried out day and night before** *You. Let my prayer come before You;* **incline Your ear to my cry.** *"* **(Psalm 88: 1-2)**

What prison are you in? What issue or challenge in life are you facing? Would you like to be set free like Peter when constant prayer was made for him (Acts 12:5)? Will you keep asking, keep seeking, and keep knocking? **There must be that inner drive and push to get through the crowd of obstruction.** It is a desperate push filled with hope. It's an attitude where we must have it or we will die.

*"And suddenly, a woman who had a flow of blood for twelve years came from behind and touched the hem of His garment for she said to herself, **"If only I may touch His garment, I shall be made well."** But Jesus turned around, and when He saw her He said, "Be of good cheer, daughter; **your faith has made you well."** And the woman was made well from that hour."* (**Mathew 9: 20-22**)

Elijah was a man of importunity as it was no feeble prayer that opened up the heavens (James 1: 15-16). What about **Moses** who prayed, fasted, and interceded for Israel for 40 days and 40 nights. **Abraham** was another classic example who pleaded with God for the sake of Sodom and Gomorrah. If he had ceased in his asking, would God have ceased in His giving?

Point to Ponder: "Whether we like it or not, asking is the rule of the Kingdom." - Charles Spurgeon

---

Jesus Christ was our example of importunity as He prayed all night on many occasions. Jesus was under the principles of prayer as He came in the flesh as our example. There would have been no transfiguration or miracles without "prayer closet" time and His importunity. If Jesus Christ the Son of God was not exempted from the rule of asking why should we?

*"I will declare the decree: **The Lord has said to Me, 'You are My Son, today I have begotten You. Ask of Me , and I will give You the nations for Your inheritance**, and the ends of the earth for Your possession."* (**Psalm 2: 7-8**)

• 12 •

TIPPING POINT – BUILDING THE PRAYER MOVEMENT

One of the purposes of this book was to help encourage 24/7/365 day and night prayer manifest in the United States. I was hoping to see a **"tipping point"** materialize where there would be a great shift in our culture. History has proven **a dedicated few can change the course of history** - for good or evil. Herrnhut (Chapter 2) was one such example of good. A few people took it upon themselves to seek God in prayer shifts which led to the "Great Awakening" and the greatest missionary move the world has ever seen.

In Russia during the Bolshevik revolution 20,000 people turned a nation of nearly 200 million to Communism. It led to Lenin and Stalin as dictators where millions of lives were taken through purges. Communism was a great evil that came upon that land and impacted the world. Just as good can come from a dedicated few - so can evil take over a nation and impact the world.

Point to Ponder: "The tipping points in history have usually come from a tiny percentage of the people. One study determined that the number of people required for a profound impact on cultural change was as few as the square root of 1% of the population. That means just 100 people can have a profound impact on a city of a million." - Rick Joyner

---

There is a call for the *radical remnant* (the dedicated elite few) to go into the prayer closet to birth a **"tipping point"**. I believe the Lord has revealed to me that personal intimate prayer time, where individuals seek the Lord daily, is the answer. I am sure there are others who feel the same way. I hope to co-labor with them and join hand-to-hand to make this vision a reality. This is the only way that a true 24/7 day and night prayer will develop. It will take individuals who feel the stirring of the Holy Spirit and the call to pray. I see the beginning already transpiring. Little prayer fires are burning across each state, and they can make a big difference especially as these fires join and burn together. The prayer movement is on the move and is becoming very contagious because of the need of the hour and the season of time we are in. A few can turn back many and can create a **"tipping point"** that moves God's hand in our behalf.

*"Ask, and it will be given to you; seek, and you will find; knock, and it will be opened to you. **For everyone who asks receives, and he who seeks finds, and to him who knocks it will be opened.** Or what man is there among you who, if his son asks for bread, will give him a stone? Or if he asks for a fish, will he give him a serpent? If you then, being evil, know how to give good gifts to your children, how much more will your Father who is in heaven **give good things to those who ask Him!*** **(Matthew 7: 7-11)**

It will take unity of the Church as well as pastors and ministries cooperating with one another to make this a reality. Division, control issues, offenses, jealousy, and all types of competition must come to an end. Jesus said a house divided will not stand. Is unity in our diversity attainable? Yes! Why not in the region where you live?

What about Divisive Politics?

It is apparent there is division in the church between various cultures such as Hispanic, White, African American, Asian churches, etc, - even in the prayer movement. Politics many times is the driving force in this division. We must forget about **the elephant** (Republican Party) and **the donkey** (Democratic Party) **but pray, vote, and choose the Lamb who became the Lion of Judah (Jesus**

Christ) and promote His Kingdom. We must think vertically (God's Kingdom) on righteousness issues. Thinking horizontally will not save our nation. When the horizontal (church) lines up with the vertical (Kingdom of God), this praying intersect is the Cross that will bring a **"tipping point"** of life and transformation!

Moving Towards the Tipping Point

Not too long ago I read a secular book called, "The Tipping Point – How Little things Can Make a Big Difference," by Malcolm Gladwell. In it I discovered a conceptual method that could be applied to the prayer movement in any state and our nation. I have come to understand how little things can make a big difference.

As I was speaking at a church one morning, I passed out matches and matchbooks to a number of individuals in the congregation. I gave three or four matches to some people. Needless to say, there was a slight stir amongst some of the ushers. I indicated that in your hand was a match that could do much good or much harm. **Each individual in that room has a sphere of influence that God has called them to impact.** If we were to light one match, the ability to light all the others in the room was there. And as I look at the state of Michigan (U.S.A. - as an example) and its 83 counties, I ask, **who are the fire starters in the prayer movement?** We are in a time when we need to pass the torch and take the sword to contend with the evil that is around us.

Point to Ponder: Can you imagine what one person can do with a match in a dry forest? One individual could burn a whole forest down. One individual with God given vision can take a city, a state, a nation!

The Verizon Network

Earlier in this book I mentioned how an individual had spoken to me and prophesied that God was going to give me a Verizon network. I was told to study those popular television commercials in my prayer closet. I clearly saw the analogy of a wireless network in our direct connection with God through prayer. We can call up God anytime!

He showed me the prayer closet movement would eliminate all "dead zones" in our state's 83 counties. We have a 3G network - the Father, the Son, and the Holy Spirit (Godhead) available to us at any time. Our friends and family are the **sphere of influence** that God has given to each of us. In the match analogy I used above, God wants us to light up those who we know in our friends and family that have a heart for prayer. Networking is what will build the prayer movement. We can carry people (friends and family) as priests of God before the throne daily for salvation of the lost.

Point to Ponder: There is a power in mobilization. Movements are catalyzed by a grass roots "few" that will grow exponentially. Find 12 good people and teach, train, and equip them to change the world. A small percentage of the population can take over a city, state or nation.

The "Tipping Point" book provided key points for me to consider helping me expedite the process. Why do major changes in our society so often happen suddenly and unexpectedly? Why do ideas, behavior, messages, and products often spread like outbreaks of infectious disease? Doesn't it take just one person who has the flu to start an epidemic? The critical mass or a social epidemic that takes place is the tipping point. **Why could we not cause a spiritual prayer epidemic in the church which would rally people into their prayer closets?** It can be done! Because of God's grace, I believe every state in the nation has individuals who are infected with a prayer contagion. In this book, the Lord showed me a roadmap we can follow in the modern-day church.

Do You See What I See?

With any flu threat, it takes only a small amount of the population (6-10%) to become infected, and in turn this would cause a pandemic. It has been proven that when any product, fad, social dilemma, or new style has taken over our culture it is because a few had infected the many. In other words, **little things can make a big difference** or **little causes have big effects**. We can understand how a few satisfied customers could end up filling the restaurant by them spreading the word. We can see the effect of television utilizing slick advertising ads with catchy phrases. Messages and behaviors can be spread just like a virus!

> **Point to Ponder:** Take a moment and think about yawning. Have you ever seen anybody yawn? Doesn't it many times make you want to yawn? Even after reading this you may have yawned and caused others to do so. We can see what the power of suggestion can do that can cause emotional contagiousness.

The "Tipping Point" book indicated there are three characteristics that need to be considered. One is *contagiousness*, the second is *little causes have big effects*, and the third one is that *changes happen not gradually but at one dramatic moment.* **Why can't those who have a heart for prayer come together to create a tipping point to bring transformation to any state or even the nation?** God is giving us the door of opportunity to step through as a perfect storm is coming upon our land. When the storm hits, it will be too late.

The Law of Geometric Progression

The book by Malcolm Caldwell explained the law of geometric progression. I immediately saw how this would work in the prayer movement. Let me take a direct quote from the introduction of his book, *"Consider, for example, the following puzzle. I give you a large piece of paper, and I ask you to fold it over once, and then take that folded paper and fold it over again, and then again, and again, until you have we folded the original paper 50 times. How tall you think the final state is going to be? In answer to that question, most people will fold the sheet in their minds eye, and guess that the pile would be as thick as a phone book or, if they are really courageous, they'll say that it would be as tall as a refrigerator. But the real answer is that the height of the stack would approximate distance to the sun. And if you fold it over one more time, the stack would be as high as the distance to the sun and back."* This is an example of what in mathematics is called a **geometric progression**.

Epidemics such as bird or swine flu (or any disease), is another example of geometric progression in operation. When a virus spreads through a population, it doubles and doubles again, until it has (figuratively) grown geometrically to infect the majority of the population. So the result of folding a single sheet of paper 50 times, one can go all the way to the sun in 50 steps."

When I read this I found it so hard to believe. But God created all the physical and natural laws in the universe - so why not the law of geometric progression? Again, let's apply this to the prayer movement!

Point to Ponder: "Intercession is truly universal work for the Christian. No place is closed to intercessory prayer. No continent - no nation - no organization - no city - no office. There is no power on earth that can keep intercession out." - Richard Halverson

---

Can You Believe With Me?

Use any state as an example. We will take this from a microcosm (church) to a macrocosm (United States). The tipping point (law of the few) **is between 6 - 10% of any population** (some say less). Each of the examples listed below I have taken approximately 8% of the total number. Remember that little things can make a big difference or little matches can cause big fires. Imagine with me that this 8% are those who have been stirred to pray and individually see the need to seek God in their prayer closet, whether on a weekly or daily basis. Let's give an example:

CREATING A TIPPING POINT TO BIRTH TRANSFORMATION!
(Using 6% - 10% - Law of the Few)

A. CHURCH of <u>100</u> PEOPLE =
   8 people praying (closet time) in that church body.

B. COUNTY WITH <u>300</u> CHURCHES =
   24 Churches taking the prayer closet seriously.

C. STATE WITH <u>80</u> COUNTIES =
5 to 8 Counties pursuing 24/7/365 Prayer.

D. UNITED STATES OF AMERICA =
5 States who actively pursue 24/7/365 Prayer.

If we can apply this concept to the prayer movement, I believe there will be a transformation of a nation. **If we can encourage 6 to 10% of the people in "the church in America" to seek God diligently in the secret place or the prayer closet, we will witness a historic move of God.** A spiritual epidemic of prayer will bring forth a **"tipping point"** and transformation of a society. Divine intervention in the cultural gateways will be a result.

Point to Ponder: Anything is possible if the task at hand is broken down into incremental steps.

Law of the Few

We must also consider three rules to a social epidemic tipping point. One is *law of the few* which we have already discussed. When 24/7 prayer is analyzed and broken down we find it is a process that can be easily accomplished. How many hours in a day? There are 24. How many ½ hour increments in a day? There are 48. How many days in a week? There are 7. How many ½ hour increments in a week? There are 336. **Can you find 336 people in your county (city) for example that will pray ½ hour a week at a designated time?** What if 136 people volunteered to take 1 hour of a designated time per week? Is there a need to encourage people to go into their prayer closets in the times we are in? Yes! Why not join counties or cities if you have a smaller population pool available?

NOTE: One may wonder about those early morning time slots. The Lord will stir the hearts of those who have been called to pray and fill the gaps. Just share the vision! What if pastors in a city begin to simultaneously preach messages on prayer? The seeds of prayer will be planted and God will do the rest.

Stickiness Factor

The second rule is the *stickiness factor*. The message regarding the importance of prayer must have this stickiness factor attached to it so people would not forget it. How we present the information will make a big difference in how much of an impact it makes. **It will take pastors, leaders in the church, and individuals who are holding the lit matches to start the fires of transformation revival.** They must see, feel, and understand the importance of prayer and carry the anointing to spread the word. The pastors are the gatekeepers of the city and must take the initial lead.

Rule of Context

The third rule is called *context*. It says **people are a lot more sensitive to their environment than they may seem**. Seeing the dire straits our nation is in is certainly a telling sign that it is the right season of time to present the prayer message with passion. If we can't see the need to pray at this time, will we ever? Will it take another national calamity or disaster? I hope not!

NOTE: Even though I have simplified some of the information in the "Tipping Point" book, I hope you can grasp the idea and concept. With God nothing is impossible. It just takes people who see the need and have that seed of vision implanted within them and walk by faith in God's purposes. Who will rise up? Is God calling you forth in your church, county or state? Will you join with me to see a prayer movement that will rise up that will not end in our nation until the Lord returns?

Modern Day Circuit Riders

Have you ever heard of the apocryphal story of the midnight ride of Paul Revere? He was a well-respected patriot and colonist who had a large sphere of influence. He received news that the British were landing on the shore and were going to make a major move. He got on his horse and decided to warn the communities surrounding Boston that the British are coming. As he rode through various towns he knocked on doors and spread the word and gave warning. Church bells began to ring and the news spread like a virus. When the British began their march, they encountered organized and fierce resistance. Paul Revere was blessed with a unique set of social gifts. How much more is the Church of Jesus Christ blessed with spiritual gifts that could be used to **sound the alarm - the enemy is on the land!** There are pastors, individuals and church leaders in cities who are the modern day Paul Reveres *(radical remnant)* - so get on your horses and ride. You are the modern day circuit riders.

Point to Ponder: Emotions are contagious. Do all that you do with passion!

One final thing that we should take note of is to respect all the connections in our sphere of influence. Some may appear to be strong while others weak. We never know who that weak connection may touch that will make a big change. We are all members of one body in Jesus Christ. Each part has an individual function and is connected to one another. We are all connectors. **Connectors are the social glue where love will lubricate and activate the joints.** Not one is to think more highly of itself than the other. As we work together as one, we will soon find the Lord will bless our efforts and command the blessing. There will be tests at times where one who has offended you holds a key link. So operate out of love and forgiveness and have a heart of restoration and reconciliation.

"Therefore if there is any consolation in Christ, if any comfort of love, if any fellowship of the Spirit, if any affection and mercy, fulfill my joy by being like-minded, having the same love, being of one accord, of one mind. **Let nothing be done through selfish ambition or conceit, but in lowliness of mind let each esteem others better than himself.** *Let each of you look out not only for his own interests, but also for the interests of others."* **(Philippians 2: 1-4)**

If you feel you are a called out one to build the prayer movement in your church, city, county, or even your state, there are a few other rules of engagement that will spare you much grief. The Holy Spirit will guide you to those who have like passions. Make sure you have listening ears as they very well may have pieces of the puzzle that you'll need in order to complete the mission.

Rules of Engagement – "A Caution in Moving Forward in Vision Fulfillment"

I attended a church gathering and an individual by the name of Tony Miller (respected church leader) taught me a principle that I learned to apply to any personal assignment from the Lord. It especially applies to building any prayer movement in your church, city, county or state. He indicated *we would encounter difficulties as we attempted to carry out the vision* that was placed within us. One of these difficulties would be the lack of agreement and passion, which could discourage us and stall our vision fulfillment. Discouragement can drain you of your spiritual energy and strength.

Point to Ponder: One of the greatest challenges in vision fulfill-ment can result in the greatest blessing. How do we get individu-als, churches, houses of prayer, ministries, and home groups to work together? We will always encounter strong personalities, and those who have personal agenda's. Do not allow this to discourage you from the vision implanted within you. Keep moving forward and network with those who have the common vision.

He spoke about how there would be five types of individuals we would encounter in our vision casting and fulfillment of the assignment given to us. I had applied this to building the prayer movement in the state I reside in. **We must learn to align with particular groups of individuals or we may lose hope and give up!** I have followed these principles even though the temptation exists to attempt to solve all the problems. I had to learn to let groups or individuals go.

1. **The Excited** – They see how you see and are passionate, because the Lord has implanted in them the same seed of vision. They are the minority but are the catalyst. (Approximately 3 - 5%)

2. **Embracers of the Vision** – These people see the potential of the vision and will certainly be supportive. (Approximately 10 - 15%)

3. **The Middlers (ones in the middle)** – This is the largest

grouping.They ride the fence and can go can go either way. They are important in the process and are needed. (Approximately 60 - 70%)

4. **Late Embracers** – This group is smaller. After they see the work in progress is having an impact, they will come on board and become late supporters of the vision. (Approximately 10 - 15%)

5. **Do Nothings** – This group is small. No matter the progress or success, they will be hardened and stubborn and never supportive because of pride, jealousy, envy, control, offenses, or other issues. (Approximately 3 - 5%)

I was taught **to focus on the excited and the embracer group**. They are the ones who would be encouraging and supportive of the vision to build a prayer movement. They would act as my delegates to win the middle group over. My role was to encourage and exhort, instill faith and confidence, so the task would be accomplished. Is it God's will that prayer increase? Yes! Can we do all things through Christ who strengthens us? Yes!

"I can do all things through Christ who strengthens me." **(Philippians 4:13)**

Point to Ponder: "Time spent in prayer will yield more than that given to work. Prayer alone gives work its worth and its success. Prayer opens the way for God Himself to do His work in us and through us. Let our chief work as God's messengers be intercession; in it we secure the presence and power of God to go with us." - Andrew Murray

---

As far as the late embracers and do nothings, they must be let go. **They would consume too much of my valuable time and spiritual energy!** I have tried to apply this principle and am so thankful for the wisdom I have been given. I found it difficult at times not to attempt to defend what I was doing (and still fail at times). We must allow the Lord to do the work and fight the battles. If the assignment you were given is of the Lord nothing will stop it

Look at Gamaliel's advice in Acts 5:

*"And now I say to you, keep away from these men and let them alone; for if this plan or this work is of men, it will come to nothing; **but if it is of God, you cannot overthrow it — lest you even be found to fight against God.**"* (**Acts 5: 38-39**)

You must call things that are not as though they were. So I hope you are encouraged by this wisdom given to me. Do not allow discouragement to set in for whatever you are called to do. **Rick Joyner (Morningstar Ministries) once stated that if something is too easy it's not worth doing anyway!** It is a faith walk no matter the degree of difficulty. God will speak to you so write down the vision (Habakkuk 2: 1-4) and pursue it with passion.

*"I will stand my watch and set myself on the rampart, and watch to see what He will say to me, And what I will answer when I am corrected. Then the Lord answered me and said: "**Write the vision and make it plain on tablets**, that he may run who reads it. For the vision is yet for an appointed time; but at the end it will speak, and it will not lie. Though it tarries, **wait for it**; because it will surely come, it will not tarry."* (**Habakkuk 2: 1-3**)

Point to Ponder: "The trouble with nearly everybody who prays is that he says 'Amen' and runs away before God has a chance to reply. Listening to God is far more important than giving Him our ideas." - Frank Laubach

---

CONCLUSION

We are facing a definite challenge as a nation. Our survival is hanging in the balance. The future lives of my children and grandchildren are at stake. I am an optimist and believe in a loving, merciful, compassionate God who wants the best for His people. God is stirring a *"radical remnant"* who believes in secret place prayer. I tried to convey in this book experiential concepts that are deep within me. I do not claim to be a proficient author but felt the need to make this book a **call** **to** **prayer**. There is an anointing that I feel that can impact lives and encourage them to pray more. In saying this, I need to grow more in the areas regarding the prayer closet. I want more of God! I realize sacrifice is necessary - our time and commitment.

I want my own children and grandchildren to know that I am fighting for them to have a future. I have been misunderstood by them at times on why I am so driven to accomplish what I feel God has laid on my heart. Running the race and finishing is my goal. I desire to see my entire family in heaven and understand this world holds nothing for me. I want to encourage my entire family to never give up but to look up as our redemption draws near.

There are many believers in the body of Christ who believe and are utilizing the methods in this publication. My hope is to inspire more people to engage in personal prayer and see an increase in the unity of the body of Christ. An army of **modern day circuit riders** must go forth in every region of our nation. Now is the time! Unified prayer will move the hand of God. There is no human remedy for the nation's challenges other than Divine intervention into our affairs. Will you answer the call today? My ears desire to hear "well done my good and faithful servant". I know you desire that for yourself and family. There is nothing else to live for but serving the one who came, died and rose again to take away the sins of the world. In Jesus name may Herrnhut come forth in America! The *Radical Remnant* is the answer.

In His Service,

Rick Warzywak

CONTACT INFORMATION:

If you would like to have Rick Warzywak speak at a conference, seminar, or church function please E-Mail or submit a request. The book provides many topical areas where aspects of prayer can be shared. A additional list of topics can be provided that can be chosen to equip and encourage the body of Christ.

Transformation Michigan
P.O. Box 12
Atlanta, MI 49709
www.TransformMI.com
preacherrick@voyager.net